the complete guide to Singapore

GW

W0007287

CFW Guidebooks
Published by CFW Publications Limited
130 Connaught Road C Hong Kong

© CFW Publications Limited, 1981
Printed in Hong Kong

PHOTO CREDITS
Keith McGreggor: Pages 4, 6, 12-13, 18, 52-53, 54, 54-55, 80, 81
Singapore Tourist Promotion Board: Pages 44, 66-67 (top), 68-69, 75
Peter Pang: Pages 48, 66-67 (middle, lower), 71 (left, top, lower right),
72, 74, 77, 78-79 (top)
Harold Stephens: Pages 68, 78, 82-83.
Hyatt Hotel: Page 94 (left).

ISBN 962 7031 05 4

the complete guide to
Singapore

By Harold Stephens

Photography: Alain Evrard

CFW GUIDEBOOKS
Hong Kong

Contents

Singapore River looking southward

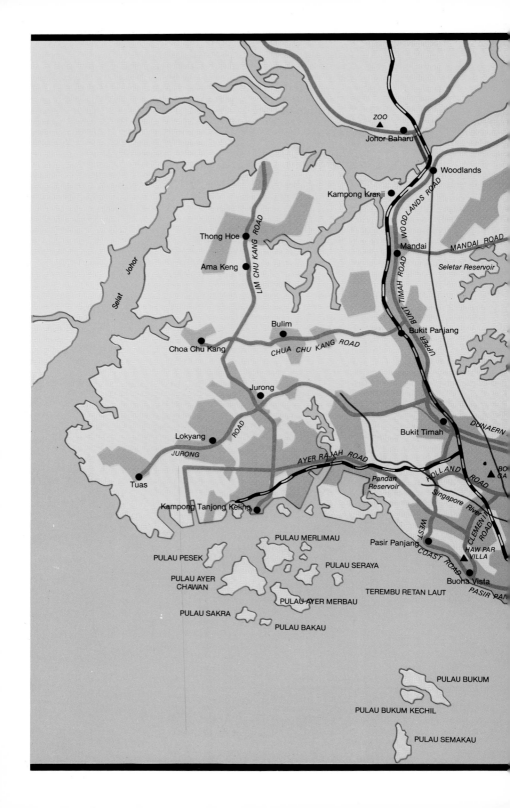

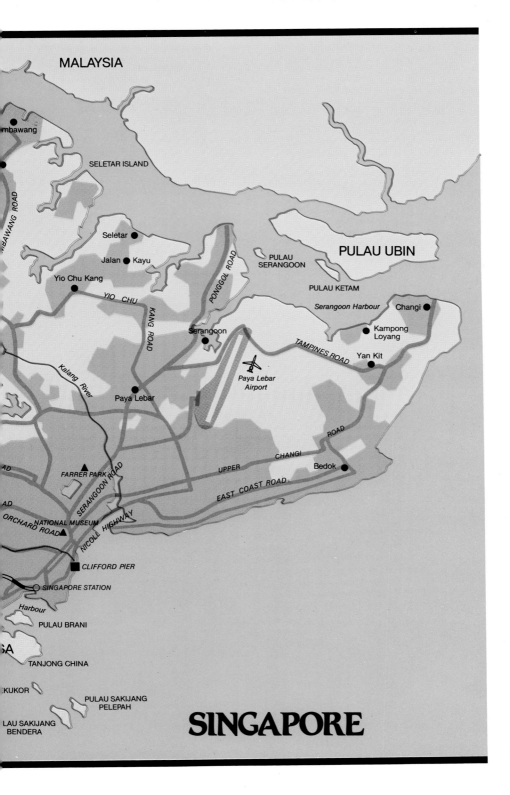

Eastern Crossroads

Ask anyone who has never been to Southeast Asia where Singapore is and chances are he or she will tell you China, or maybe Malaysia, or Indonesia. Geographically Singapore could be any one of these. Look at a map and you will see this island republic is situated at the crossroads of East and West and serves as the gateway to all Southeast Asia. Indonesia is so near that many of its islands are visible on the horizon. Malaysia is linked to Singapore by the **Johore Causeway**, a road and rail bridge that takes only minutes to cross. And to the north and northeast only a step farther are Thailand and the Philippines, and beyond them, China.

When we think of Singapore, we think of a pulsating, Oriental port. But Singapore is more. Singapore is Singapore City, situated on Singapore Island, and consists of 52 smaller islands, some a mere few acres in size. The total land area is 602 sq km. Singapore Island is 42 km. long and 23 km. wide and has a 133 km. coastline.

What surprises most visitors is that Singapore, being only 136 km. north of the Equator, has some very pleasant weather. It's warm and sunny every day but average temperatures seldom rise above 23.5° C (74.5° F). Nor is there a distinct wet or dry season, although most rainfall does occur during the Northeast Monsoon from November to January. The showers are usually sudden and heavy but also brief and refreshing.

Singapore's strategic location — where the Indian Ocean and the South China Sea meet and where one monsoon ends and another begins — made it what it is today. The history of Singapore begins with man's early migrations and, later, with trade.

From Songkok to Solar Topee to Independence

Singapore's earliest history is so sketchy it must be left to the anthropologists to interpret. But they do tell us that man began his migrations down the Malay Peninsula more than eight centuries ago and, most likely, Singapore was the stepping stone to the south. The first Western observers in the area were Arab seafarers and traders who arrived between the 10th and 16th centuries. They probably wrote what was the first guide book to Southeast Asia when they named island landmarks other vessels were to follow. Much of Singapore's early history is legend based on fact. It begins in the 11th century. We know for certain the island — which we call Singapore today — was originally known to the Malays as *Temasek*, meaning "Sea Town." The legend begins when a Sumatran prince from Palembang was on a hunting trip and sailed among the islands looking for game, and when he reached Temasek he thought he saw a lion on the bank of the river. This was a good omen. He renamed the island *Singa Pura*, Malay-Sanskrit words meaning Lion City, and built a trading empire that flourished for 200 years — "the Constantinople of the Eastern Seas," as one writer put it. But in 1377 a Javanese ruler, the Rajah of Majapahut, conquered *Singa Pura* and laid waste to the port. After its fall, the once important Lion City reverted to a small fishing village and for more than 400 years was a haunt for pirates. But *Singa Pura* wasn't forgotten. Admiral Cheng Ho sailed through the harbour with a fleet of 86 junks and 37,000 men in 1433 on his way home to China. In 1595 the Dutch explorer Jan Huyghen drew up the first detailed charts of *Singa Pura* and the neighbouring islands. James Weddel was the next cartographer to sail over the horizon and a few years later the

Singapore River looking down from the United Overseas Banking Building

buccaneer William Dampier arrived on the scene and gave the local pirates a taste of competition.

Although Singapore's early beginnings may remain the subject of considerable speculation, we are certain about Singapore's modern history. It began with Sir Thomas Stamford Raffles.

Raffles was searching for a suitable port to establish a trading post for the British East India Company. He reached *Singa Pura* in 1819 and dropped anchor at the mouth of a river. On the right bank he found the remnants of a Malay fortress, where there stood a block of sandstone weirdly engraved. (It could well have become the "Rosetta Stone" to Singapore's early history, but unfortunately it was destroyed before any attempts were made to decipher it). Scattered along the shore was something else. "There were hundred of human skulls," Raffles wrote in his journal. "Some of them old, some of them with hair still remaining, some with teeth still sharp and some without teeth."

The skulls were probably the heads of pirate victims or pirates themselves who came up-river and fought among themselves while dividing their spoils. But the graves and threats of pirates did not

Above, *Sir Stanford Raffles, founder of Singapore and* right, *Loading rubber into barges along Boat Quay, Singapore River*

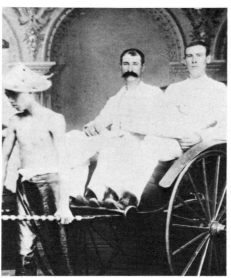

Singapore a free port, exempt from customs and excise duties, and invited merchants from every trading station from Siam to India and from China to the Moluccas Islands to engage in the entrepôt trade. Immediately, merchants and traders began to arrive, and each tide brought more people — Chinese, Indians, Eurasians, Europeans — merchant, labourer, tradesman, clerk, businessman, buyer and seller, all who came to serve the trade. They came and began to build, shops and storehouses, riverside godowns, places of worship, residences and government houses, and progress bred more trade, and more trade brought more people. Traffic from harbour to river grew in leaps and bounds. A mere six months after Raffles established Singapore as a free port the population had grown to 5,000. Four years later there were 10,000 inhabitants.

deter Raffles from founding a trading post. The geographic location of the island was excellent, and the river offered good anchorage with surf free unloading.

Raffles signed a treaty with the Sultan of Johore giving him the right to establish a trading post. Raffles declared

Top, *Japanese surrender October, 1945;* bottom, *pre-war visitors to Singapore enjoy a rickshaw ride and* right, *bumboats and barges on the Singapore River*

During the years 1823 to 1826, Singapore was under the direct control of the British Governor-General in India. Along with Malacca and Penang, Singapore became part of the *Straits Settlement*, governed from Bengal. Finally, in 1867, the *Straits Settlement* became a crown colony.

In 1845 the first scheduled service between Singapore and Southampton began when Lady Mary Wood, a paddle-wheel steamer of 553 tons, steamed into **Singapore Harbour**. But an even bigger impetus to trade and expansion came with the opening of the Suez Canal in 1869. It shortened the trade route between Europe and Asia and freight charges decreased. Singapore's progress and prosperity gained rapid momentum and continued uninterrupted, even during World War I, until one Monday morning on February 16, 1942. Uninvited Japanese troops entered the city shortly after dawn and remained in occupation for three and a half years.

The war brought to Singapore sudden and far-reaching social changes. The Japanese fostered racial tension and under their harsh rule the Chinese suffered the hardest. When Japan surrendered it meant an Allied victory in the Pacific but to the Singaporeans it was an exchange of one master for another. They began their struggle for independence.

Self government was granted by Great Britain in 1948. From 1963 to 1965 Singapore was a member state of the Federation of Malaysia, but after differences of opinion it separated from the Federation on August 9, 1965.

As an independent sovereign nation, Singapore was admitted to the United Nations on September 21, 1965. In December the same year she became a republic headed by a president.

It is difficult to imagine pre-Raffles Singapore when you stand on the Cavanagh Bridge and look down at the bumboats and lighters plying the river.

From the 150 inhabitants Raffles found on the island when he arrived, Singapore has grown to more than two and quarter million people, and has established herself as the world's third largest port. It's Asia biggest emporium and largest storehouse of goods. Statistics are staggering. Some 43,000 ships arrive each year, with an average of 240 ship arrivals and departures daily. A ton of cargo is handled every minute of the working day, of which one third is destined for the Singapore River. And Singapore is home for a dozen different races all living under one flag. Singapore, from Raffles to the present, has come a long way indeed.

The Colonial Heritage

"In a world in which it is becoming increasingly fashionable for newly independent countries to erase the name of past father figures from their newly printed history books, to topple their statues, to speak of them only with contempt, it is refreshing to find the name of one white man, long since dead, still regarded with respect by the independent country he founded. The man is Sir Thomas Stamford Raffles, the country is the small, prosperous, idyllic island-state of Singapore." The *Singapore Story* by Noel Barber, Fontana/Collins, London.

After a hundred and sixty-one years the name Raffles is still synonymous with Singapore. There is the famous colonial landmark, the **Raffles Hotel**, and along the waterfront is Raffles Quay. The very centre of the downtown banking and shopping centre is known as **Raffles Place**. And a tourist site along the river is marked **Raffles Landing**, where there stands a larger-than-life statue of Sir Stamford Raffles, staring out over the Singapore River. And many old timers still call the **National Museum** "Raffles Museum".

Traditional river craft left *and colonial style elegance survive in modern Singapore*

Singapore was Raffles' dream, but he was only able to visit the settlement three times, the visits totalling no more than one year. His time was well spent. He framed a complete set of laws to govern the new colony. He encouraged immigration and permitted freedom of worship. In fact, he gave $3,000 to help build the first Moslem mosque, which is now in the heart of **Chinatown**. Raffles outlawed slavery — "No individual can hereafter be imported for sale, transfer or sold as a slave or slave-debtor." He granted freedom to all. He banned cock fighting and brothels and gambling houses. He founded **Raffles College**, ordered the first bridge to be built across the river, established a land registry and laid out the plans for the city. He was meticulous in every way, and in a sense he was responsible for much of the style of older architecture we see around Singapore today. "All houses constructed of brick and tile, " he wrote to the town planning committee on November 4, 1822, "should have a uniform type of front, each having a verandah of certain depth, open at all times as a continuous and covered passage on each side of the street."

From the very start Singapore became an "English" town. British merchants and civil servants brought their wives and families from England, and in a short time made for themselves an easy life which they could not have found back home. They had an abundance of servants and filled their residences with unsuitable heavy furniture and other impractical reminders of home. They had shipped out from England, via the Cape, their family paintings, Belgian carpets, oak poster beds and inlaid sideboards, all upon which the mildew of the tropics thrived and the voracious white ants feasted. Life was made easier when steamers began their regular monthly service between Singapore and Britain

Top, bottom, *Empress Place;* centre, *old facade in Chinatown;* right, *Trengganu Street in Chinatown*

and home leave was assured.

The Englishman in Singapore prided himself with "working hard and playing hard," but he also insisted upon living comfortably. One army officer, perhaps boastfully, wrote home: "Even a moderate family keeps a butler, two under-servants, a maid, a cook with an assistant, a washerman, two grooms, a grass cutter, a sweeper and a waterman." He concluded that like all fellow officers he had his private barber who came each morning to shave him.

Social life centred around private dinner parties at home, band concerts on the **Padang** and Saturday nights at "the club". Dress and proper etiquette were important. At home, with *punkah* fans swinging overhead, men dressed in dinner jackets and boiled white shirts and women in long, high-necked brocaded dresses and white gloves. They ate heavy European meals of roast beef and mutton and potatoes followed by plates of rice and curry. Afterwards came English "pudding." Meals rarely varied.

Opposite: *Urban-renewal along North Bridge Road*, above, *Moslem Indian at Upper Serangoon Road*

But there was a price to pay for the good life. Malaria, dysentery and dengue fever were a constant threat. Hospitals were primitive, and each time a new shipment of immigrants arrived from China there might well follow an epidemic of smallpox or cholera. For many years, Singapore had no quarantine station and these human cargoes brought leprosy and filariasis and a multitude of other dreadful Asian diseases. As late as 1902, 759 people in one year died of cholera.

Another menace, as unbelievable as it might seem today, was tigers. Tigers took, on the average, one Chinese coolie a day. The last tiger to be shot was in 1931. Rudyard Kipling used his literary license when he visited Singapore in 1889 and wrote that two years before his arrival the headmaster of the Raffles Institute was playing billiards in Raffles Hotel when a mighty roar caused him to miscue. There was a tiger under the billiard table. Kipling was obviously impressed by what he saw in Singapore. He found "five solid miles of masts and funnels along the waterfront."

Raffles Hotel, with or without tigers

23

under the billard table, was the social centre for colonial Singapore and continued so until the new hotels with their fancy supperclubs and cocktail lounges began to spring up along **Orchard Road** in recent years. The hotel, along with the E & O Hotel in Penang and The Strand in Rangoon, was purchased by three Armenian brothers named Starkie. It was soon noted as "The Savoy of the East." The Raffles Hotel is still a grand place to lounge in deep rattan chairs while listening to old-timers talk about the good old days before tourists when servants were reliable and people watched polo matches rather than television. And as it always has been, Raffles on Sunday morning is the place to go for coffee after church services at the Cathedral across the way on the Padang.

Singapore's economy spurred, and a new breed of adventurers came East when the world began to clamour for tin and rubber. The plantation in Singapore and Malaya to the north now became the focal point of colonial life. By carving up the jungle, fortunes could be made, but the work was extraordinarily difficult and it took years before profits were seen.

Those who could survive the disease and heat returned to England and retired in comfort.

Until World War II, the English were the privileged class. Basically they remained pretty well divided from other races. The Englishman had a rigid code of rules he had to follow.

Custom and tradition dictated his everyday life. For example, if he married an Asian girl he was ostracized from his own society. Children from such marriages were barred from British schools and clubs and from participating in sports, and no matter how accomplished in business they were, they could only earn half the salary of their counterparts.

The British influence is seen everywhere in Singapore today. The education and legal systems are British. Much of the architecture is Victorian. Motorists drive on the left side of the road, tiffin is served in hotels, and when wealthy Chinese educate their sons they prefer to send them to Cambridge and Oxford. And you can still watch polo twice a week at **Thompson Road**.

24

The Cultural Heritage

Seventy-six percent of Singapore's population is Chinese, but you can't call a Singaporean "Chinese." He is either Hokkien, Teochew, Hakka or Cantonese. Nor can you say he is Indian, for he may be Tamil, Bengali, Sikh or Pakistani. He may also be Malay, Indonesian, Brit or any other of a dozen sects or races. The Singaporean will tell you he belongs to a multi-racial community, which is another way of saying Singapore is a conglomorate of races living in a polyglot society.

But whatever he may be, the Singaporean prides himself on being Singaporean; yet on the other hand he strongly adheres to racial ties. The reason is deeply rooted in Singapore's cultural heritage. When Raffles invited people from all races to come and engage in trade in the newly founded colony, immigrants came, but not with the idea of remaining forever. Each group brought their life-style with them and had no intention of joining another culture. Besides, there wasn't any culture to join. Singapore then was only an idea, a place for opportunity. The Chinese came to earn money to send back home, and to eventually return to China with a full purse. The Indian came to serve as trooper or guard, or, for the convicts, to serve out a sentence. The Malays came to trade and sail back home. Even the Englishman's dream was to return to

Faces of Singapore, Chinese, Indian labourer, Indian girls on Sentosa, smiling Indian worker, and Chinese Samfoo woman

England when he retired. What resulted was a most unique society, each racial group living side by side with one another but following their own customs, knowing they must tolerate their neighbours if they wanted to get along.

Nearly all Chinese immigrants in the 19th century came from South China. The most numerous were the Hokkiens who, from the start, dominated Singapore's commercial life. Next were the Teochews who competed with the Hokkiens. The Cantonese and Hakkas came as agricultural labourers, tin miners and artisans — tailors, goldsmiths and carpenters. Today, 42 per cent of the Chinese population is Hokkien, with half that number of Teochews. The Cantonese are in the minority at 17 percent.

When Raffles arrived there were 120 Malays and 30 Chinese living on the island. The Chinese born in Singapore became known as Straits-born Chinese and, like the British, were members of a privileged class. Many became British subjects under a naturalisation law passed in 1852. They held the best jobs and lived in the finest houses in town. When more and more China-born immigrants arrived, they moved into the outskirts of town. Many of their homes can still be seen on **Emerald Hill** and **Cuppage Road**.

The Malay population expanded and mixed freely with Javanese and Sumatran immigrants, and with others of the Riau Archipelago. Today, out of every 50 Singaporeans, seven are Malay.

Indians came as labourers and traders, garrison troops and later as convicts. The majority were from south India. Like the Chinese, the young men worked hard and lived frugally to save enough money to return home one day. Not until after 1860 did Indian women begin to arrive. Indian convict labourers were allowed a great deal of freedom. **St. Andrew's**

From top: *Sikh watchman, bumboat attendant, pious pedler.* Opposite *Chinese students avidly reading English language newspapers*

Church and many other government buildings were built by them.

More than three-fourths of Singapore's population lives in government-built high-rise flats. Many of these self-contained building complexes and housing estates form satellite cities scattered around the island. But don't think that all Singapore is high-rise and urban living. Some 45,000 farmers live on the west side of the island. The rural area covers nearly 200 square kilometres with a population of more than half a million. Most of the population on the smaller islands, mainly fishermen, have also been relocated into housing flats. Only a few Malay-style *kampongs* exist, and even their days are numbered.

Singapore today is a country of youth on the move. More than half the population is under 20 years of age. For a country with no resources, the hard-working, industrious Singaporeans have created an economic miracle that astounds the world. They enjoy the highest per capita income in Asia after Japan. Singapore has become the third busiest port and has replaced Hong Kong as the financial centre. The country has no unemployment, no beggars, no drug problem and very little crime. And aside from being the biggest warehouse in Asia, Singapore became Southeast Asia's biggest workshop. And, what everyone will agree, Singapore is Asia's cleanest city. You can eat anywhere, at the smallest roadside stall, and have no need to worry. But don't throw a cigarette butt on the sidewalk. It could mean a $50 fine. It does help to keep the streets clean.

Singapore's multi-racial society makes it an interesting place for the visitor. Fitting is the name "Instant Asia" that she has been dubbed.

Clockwise from top left, Malay school boys, two young Indian brothers, Chinese boys, former Mr. Singapore, Chinese girls, Malay youth

The Tourist Trail

Have you ever visited another country, spent a few days and left feeling you really got to know the place? Then, back home, a friend mentions some insignificant tourist spot you didn't see and tells you how "absolutely marvellous" it was. You suddenly feel you really missed out. It's always the case. If you don't want that to happen in Singapore, here is a check-list of attractions that "shouldn't be missed." On the other hand, if you want to see and do something different, that too is possible. For those who want a bit of adventure see the section on "Off the Beaten Track."

What You Should See

There's a 45-minute show in Singapore that can give you an introduction to the city and its history, culture and people that would take you weeks to accomplish on your own. In fact, there are people who live in Singapore who, once they see the show, are amazed at what they themselves missed or didn't know. The place is the **Singapore Cultural Theatre** on Grange Road, near the Singapore Handicraft Centre. There are seven shows every day from 12 noon to 6 pm. The price is $5. Remember, it's an introduction to Singapore that will help you better understand what is to come. Also at the theatre, at 9:45 am. daily, is the cultural show "Instant Asia". This certainly has to be the best bargain in town for $5. Dancing and costumes are excellent, and you can't help finding an affectionate spot in your heart for the loveable lady lion with blinking eyelashes in the Lion Dance. Also shown are Malay, Chinese and Indian folk dances, with some very lovely lady performers, and from the audience comes an Indian snake charmer with two huge snakes, which he informs the audience, are "not very harmful and never bite". The shows are sponsored by the Singapore Tourist Promotion Board (STPB).

Botanic Gardens. Nassim Road
This is a nature trip in a true tropical garden. Gone are tigers and even monkeys but you have graceful swans to feed and gorgeous rare orchids to admire. You can stroll amid avenues of trees and relax by a miniature lake and pavilion. If you are interested in primeval jungles, the oldest on this planet, the Botanic Gardens will interest you. Daily 6 am. to 10 pm., Saturday and Sunday till midnight. Admission free.

Chinatown. Between South Bridge and New Bridge Roads, west of Singapore River
So much has been written and said about Singapore's Chinatown that the area has become world known. The pity is that with urban renewal there's not much of it left. **Death Street** (Sago Lane) is gone, and most of the old Chinese baroque shophouses are abandoned. But still, see it while you can. The best way is to take a

Dancers from the Singapore Cultural Theatre. Clockwise from top left, Indian, Malay, Indian and Chinese lion and attendant

street map and wander about at leisure, stopping to admire the darkened doorways and peak into all the sundry shops. For more information on exploring Chinatown see the section "Off the Beaten Track".

Chinese Chamber of Commerce Building. Hill Street
This is as close as you can come to Beijing (Peking). It's a spectacular treat for your camera! Nine Dragons Walls at the entrance is an exact duplicate of the famous wall at Beijing's Imperial Palace.

Crocodile Farms. Upper Serangoon Road
The farm is more interesting than it may sound. If you've never seen an eight-foot-long crocodile suddenly snap at a fish tossed over its head, then you have a surprise awaiting you. They are as quick as a lightning. Find out how crocodiles are raised. Learn to choose good quality crocodile skin items for which Singapore is famous. Arrange for a visit through a travel agent or by calling the STPB.

Japanese Garden and Yu Hwa Yuan Chinese Garden. Jurong

Singaporeans love their gardens, and none are more popular than the Japanese and Chinese gardens in Jurong. Each ranges over 13 hectares on adjacent man-made islands in **Jurong Lake**. This is a unique opportunity to contrast Japanese and Chinese landscaping and architectural styles. Both open daily 9 am. to 10 pm. (no admission after 9 pm). Japanese Garden admission 80 cents, children half price. Chinese Garden admission: $1.50, 80 cents children. Combined admission $2.00, children $1.00

Jurong Bird Park. Jurong

Singapore can rightfully boast of having the world's largest bird park. It was built mainly as a tourist attraction but it's the Singaporeans who enjoy it more than anyone. The collection is complete, from arctic dwellers to birds-of-paradise, vultures to flamingoes, over 7,000 birds of more than 350 species. See some in mock-natural habitats, other flying free in the 2-hectare netted **Falls Aviary** where a 30-metre waterfall thunders beneath Rainbow Bridge. Tour on foot or by tramcar; open from 9 am. to 6:30 pm. on weekdays, and from 9 am. to 7 pm. on weekends and public holidays. Admission $2.50; children $1.00.

Kranji Cemetery and War Memorial. Woodsland Road

The beauty of the cemetery is unsurpassed, but the mood can be heavy. Most visitors are returning World War II veterans. Nonetheless, it's a moving tribute to those who died in Southeast Asia during the war.

34

Mandai Gardens. Mandai Lake Road
Anyone from America or Europe would
have a hard time imagining four hectares
of orchids! But there they are. The
gardens are a mind-bender for anyone
who ever thought an orchid spells
tropical romance. See rare Malaysian
blooms and exotic new hybrids. There's a
tropical water garden, too. Daily 9 am. to
6 pm. Admission $1.00; children and
tour group members 50 cents.

Markets. Sungei Road and Chinatown
Want to buy an old iron, the kind you
have to put hot coals inside to heat up?
What about an old cannon, or a ship's
lantern? Or lamps or books — or
anything? The secret to shopping the
markets is not being afraid to look. You
might get dirty but the finds could be
worth it. Singapore's junk shops have just
about anything and everything. They call
them "Thieves' Markets" but Singapore
has few thieves nowadays. The only
thievery is the high prices you might have
to pay. But fun can be had in the
haggling. Try **Sungei Road** along the
canal and, when the sun goes down,
venture down to the night market in
Chinatown. It's safe.

Mt. Faber. Off Telok Blangah (Pasir
Panjang) Road
Want to see a glorious tropical sunset?
Mt. Faber is the place. The view any time
of the day or night is excellent. Mt. Faber
is one of the highest points in Singapore.
You can get an eagle's eye view of city,
harbour, sea and the islands beyond.

National Museum. Stamford Road
The attic is rumoured to be haunted,
according to most Chinese, but it's
closed anyway to the public. See the
famous Haw Par collection of jade
displayed on the first floor. It's worth
millions. Other exhibits vary from
prehistoric archaeology to Malay
weapons, silverware and fabrics, Chinese
export porcelain, and regional currency.

Chimpanzee at Singapore Zoo; right *and*
bottom, *Jurong Bird Park, hornbill,
garden, parrot and walk through park
with net overhead*

Also West Malaysian aborigines'
material and Chinese furniture and
costumes. Daily 10:30 am. to 7 pm. Free
film shows, Wednesdays 8 pm.

Sentosa Island

Best two-dollar bargain in town. It gets
you a ferry ride there and back, free
admission to most of the island's
attractions and free bus transportation.
Join the Singaporeans having fun, but
avoid the rush during weekends and
holidays. The coralarium has one of the
finest collections of coral, shells and
marine life in Southeast Asia. The
Maritime Museum will fascinate the
history buff with models and
photographs of many vessels, old and
new. **Fort Siloso** can give you an idea of
what the defences of "impregnable"
Singapore were like prior to World War
II. All the guns pointed to sea. The
Japanese came from the rear, down the
Peninsula. The impressive Surrender
Chamber puts you on the scene in 1945
when the Japanese gave Singapore back.
There's also a man-made swimming
lagoon, a natural sand beach and an 18-

hole golf course.

You can reach Sentosa via ferry from Platform 2, **World Trade Centre**, or by cable car from **Jardine Steps** or Mt. Faber. Cable car riders pay Sentosa admission fees on arrival. Ferry passengers can buy, at World Trade Centre, tickets at $4 adults, $2 children under 18, covering ferry rides, Sentosa entry fee, admission to all the above, free

soft drink, guide book and rides on all buses. Adult $2 tickets (children $1) entitle you to same transport and sightseeing except for Coralarium admission, soft drink and guide book. Bus services operate 9:30 am. to 6:30 pm. daily and from 8 am. Sunday and holidays.

Science Centre. Jurong

Here's some educational fun for all ages. There are 322 exhibits and pushbutton demonstrations which cover physical and life sciences, from nuclear power to

Looking eastward toward Katong, most of the which area has been reclaimed

human birth. Open 10 am to 6 pm, Tuesdays through Sundays. Closed Mondays except for public holidays. Admission $1, 50 cents children.

Singapore Handicraft Centre. Grange Road

If you expect a handicraft centre to be a rough-hewn building where local artists and craftsmen have set up shop, then you'll be disappointed with the Singapore Handicraft Centre. It's all concrete and glass and even has a red carpet or two, and not always do you see local artisans at work. But it is interesting if you want to see a wide collection of handicrafts from countries as far away as The Philippines, or as close as Malaysia. Some 30 shops show off their products. Sometimes there are free folkloric shows in the centre's internal plaza.

Tiger Balm Gardens. Haw Par Villa, Pasir Panjang Road

Kids love it. Adults find it amusing, and nearly every tourist who comes to Singapore goes there. It's Asia's Disneyland of still-life replicas of animals and an outdoor horror museum of bizarre statues from Chinese mythology, including lurid depictions of puragatory. Open from 10 am to 6 pm. Admission free.

Van Kleef Aquarium. Clemenceau Avenue

If you plan to go scuba diving in the waters around Singapore you might check out the Van Kleef Aquarium first to see what's in store for you. You may change your mind. Moray eels, sharks, water snakes, only to name of few of the 4,000 specimens of fish and sea life on display. Open daily from 9:30 to 9 pm. Admission 60 cents, 40 cents for children.

Zoological Gardens. Mandai Road

Many of Singapore's and Malaysia's indigenous animals live here in an environment as close as possible to their natural surroundings. The park is set on

28.3 hectares (70 acres) of thick wooded hills. Some 1,250 animals of 130 species inhabit this beautiful setting. You can follow jungled walks reaching out into **Seletar Reservoir**. Open 8:30 am. to 6 pm. daily. Animal "Show Time" is at 11 am. and 3 pm. Admission $2.50, $1.20 for children. Slight extra charge for cameras.

Joining a Tour

Joining a tour is the quickest and surest way of getting to know Singapore. Afterwards you can return at your own leisure to those places you most favoured. The STPB has organised several such tours to better help tourists appreciate Singapore with as much case as possible.

OUR PEOPLE, OUR HERITAGE is a tour of **Chinatown, Little Indian** on Serangoon Road and **Thieves Market** on Arab Street. THE RAFFLES CONNECTION TAKES THE VISITOR TO THE **National Museum**, Raffles Hotel, Boat Quay, the Raffles Landing Site and a final visit at the **Singapore Cultural Theatre** to view an extravagant electronic slide show "The Singapore Experience." OUR CRAFTS And ARTS begins with a tour of the **Singapore Handicraft Centre** following a visit to a crocodile farm, a batik factory, a pewter-making factory and a gemcutting factory. THE MINI RIVER CRUISE AND KATONG DISCOVERY is a journey into the past. If you blank

---

Opposite, *Chinese warrior fighting fabled lion in Tiger Balm Gardens and* above, *swimming lagoon at tourist complex on Sentosa Island*

out the high rises in the background you could be in Singapore a hundred years ago. It's a 45-minute cruise up the Singapore River by bumboat followed by a visit to the **Kampong Arang Boatyard** and a Malay village. DAYBREAK OF AN AWAKENING CITY is an unusual tour but only for those who like to rise early, and haven't done **Bugis Street** the night before. The tour begins in the **Central Vegetable Market** at Carpenter Street, and leads to Chinatown and Boat Quay with a "buk kut teh" breakfast at River Valley Road. GARDENS OF SINGAPORE is a back to nature tour of the Botanic Gardens, Toa Payoh and Siong Lim Gardens, MacRitchie Reservoir and Central Park. Several travel agents operate these tours. Check with the STPB for more information.

Singapore has no waterfront drive or harbour-side restaurants that give residents and visitors a view of the harbour. Yet the harbour is so vitally important to Singapore. The only way you can get a feeling for this world's third largest port is to hire a private launch or bumboat, or join one of the three standard water tours. These are the DAY-TIME HARBOUR CRUISE, THE EVENING JUNK CRUISES, and the SENTOSA, SOUTHERN ISLAND TOUR. Don't miss the waterfront and harbour.

Religion for Everyone

Singaporeans enjoy complete freedom of worship, and they are strong followers of their individual faiths. The main religions are Buddhism, Islam, Christianity, Hinduism and Taoism. Other religious groups include the Sikhs, Jews, Jains and Zoroastrians. Singapore's places of worship are both architectual and historical sites of importance. You can freely enter Buddhist temples and Islamic mosques, providing you leave your shoes outside the mosque. Some temples are huge and cover an area the size of a city block, while others are modest curbside shrines. The churches are interesting not only for their architectural design but for the history related on plaques hung on

church house walls. The following are some of the more important and interesting temples, mosques and churches.

Al-Abrar Mosque. Telok Syer Street, Chinatown
The mosque is Tamil and goes by many different names. It was originally built in 1827 when Telok Ayer Street was a beach front. The original mosque was replaced by a brick one in 1850.

Armenian Church. Hill Street
This is the oldest Christian church in Singapore, built in 1835 when there were only twelve Armenian families in town. Services no longer take place here and the church is preserved as an historic landmark.

Chettiar Hindu Temples. Tank Road
A very active place during the exotic Thaipusan festival in January each year. The temple was built in 1850 and dedicated to Lord Subramaniam, the six-headed Hindu god.

Two larger-than-life statues in Haw Par Villa, better known as Tiger Balm Gardens

Hajjah Fatimah Mosque. Java Road
Built around 1845, this small but
picturesque Moslem Mosque has a
leaning minaret. The mosque was built by
a Malay lady who came from Malacca
and married a Bugis merchant trading in
Singapore. It reflects the architecture
found in Malacca.

Leong San Temple. Race Course Road
Also known as Dragon Mountain
Temple, it is dedicated to the Goddess of
Mercy, Kuan Yin. Only people with a
pure heart and mind, and who abstain
from strong drink and meat, may enter
the temple.

Hong San Temple. Mohammed Sultan
Road
The temple was built by the wealthy
Chinese who came from Fukkien
province in China. They are among the
richest people in Singapore. The temple,
which has been restored, is one of the
most beautiful in the city.

Saint Andrews Cathedral. Coleman
Street
A major landmark in Singapore, this
Anglican Cathedral was built in the early
English Gothic style between 1856 and
1863 by Indian convict labour. It's
centrally located near the **Padang**.

Siong Lim Temple. Jalan Tao Payoh
A Buddhist temple with elaborate wood
carvings reminiscent of palaces in Beijing
(Peking) and pillars sculptured with
dragons and phoenixes. In front is a
garden of pure white limestone boulders.

Sivan Temple. Orchard Road
Second oldest place of Hindu worship in
Singapore. The temple dates back to
1850 and was entirely reconstructed in
1964. The statues on the *gopuram*, or
tower, at the entrance represent Siva, the
third god of the Indian Trinity. Friday
evening is the time to watch the service.

Sri Mariamman Temple. South Bridge
Road
This is the oldest Hindu Temple in
Singapore, built between 1827 and 1843,
and without doubt is also the most
photographed, with its colourful and

flamboyantly decorated tower.

Sultan Mosque. North Bridge Road
The biggest and most popular mosque in
Singapore. Try to pay a visit at noon on
Fridays, the Moslem sabbath. The chant
of the Muezzin calls the faithful to
prayers as barefoot male followers kneel
on wall-to-wall carpeting on the cool
marble floor. Incongruous are digital
clocks which show the times in Singapore
and in the Holy City of Mecca.

Temple of 1000 Lights. Race Course Road
Known as the Buddha Gaya Temple, it's
an interesting mixture of both Chinese
and Indian culture. A 15-metre
statue of Buddha surrounded by
countless lights which are lit on festivals,
dominates the temple. There is a replica
of Buddha's footprint and a piece of bark
from the original Bodhi tree.

Thian Hock Keng Temple. Telok Ayer Street
The Temple of Heavenly Happiness is
important to Hokkien Taoists. Dwarfed
by downtown buildings surrounding it, its
granite pillars and ornamental stonework,
wood carvings and the image of the deity
were all transported from China in 1840.

Singapore Bargains and Treasures

It's a broad statement but it's true. In
Singapore you can buy anything! With
43,000 ships loading and unloading their
wares each year, the port has to be an
international warehouse and shopping
emporium for any need. Where else can
you buy a second-hand satelite tracking
station, an oil well rig, a floating dock, a

Top, *Moslem prayers at the Sultan
Mosque;* bottom left, *Hindu worshipers,*
bottom right, *Onion Dome of the Sultan
Mosque*
Over: left, *Devotee at Kuan Lim Goddess of
Mercy Temple on Waterloo Street*
top right, *Kong Meng San Phor Kark See
Temple on Bright Hill Drive;* bottom right,
*Sattha Puchaniyaram Temple on Holland
Road*

43

shiny new yacht, half a million tons of
raw rubber or 20,000 board feet of
timber. Few visitors ever see these sales
and transactions, but they go on, day in
and day out. But not all buyers are
looking for oil rigs or timber. For the
other shopper, the tourist, Singapore
offers her own special bargains at rates
seen no where else in Asia; — cameras,
watches, calculators, stereo equipment
and Persian carpets. All are sold duty-
free which makes prices among the
lowest in the word. Electrical goods and
home appliances are also available at
duty-free prices. You can find many
kinds of Oriental treasure, from antiques
to zircons, cheaper in Singapore than in
most other Asian countries, including
countries of origin. The law forbids shops
to hang "duty-free" signs so there's no
fear of false advertising.

Most shops open at 10:00 am. and
don't close until 9:30 pm. every day. On
Orchard Road alone, there are several
shopping complexes with over 100
speciality shops each, department stores
occupying three or more floors,
boutiques, and low-priced Chinese
emporiums. Other shopping areas are at
Raffles Place and the **North Bridge Road**
and **High Street** area. For a completely
different kind of shopping experiences,
visit the street bazaars of Chinatown and
Thieves Market.

Haggling is expected, and they say it's
only a fool who pays the first price
quoted. If you are good, with plenty of
tears, you can get as much as 30 percent
off the price. Even in expensive shops
with prices marked and supposedly fixed,
try to get at least your 10 percent.

Shopping Complexes

Once "not so long ago" the average
Singaporean did his shopping along the
arcaded street of North Bridge Road and
Chinatown, at the bazaar in **Change
Alley** and at night markets scattered
around town. Then came urban renewal.
One of the first super shopping
complexes to appear was **People's Park**.

Before long, air conditioned complexes rose up all over town, from the dust where old shophouses stood only a few months before. The list of shopping complexes here is not complete, for new centres appear faster than Singapore's legendary "four-legged snake" changes colour. Places to go:

Change Alley Aerial Plaza, Collyer Quay
Columbo Court, North Bridge Road
Cuppage Road Shopping Centre, Cuppage Road
Far East Shopping Centre, Orchard Road
The Gallery, Battery Road
High Street Centre, North Bridge Road
The Orchard, Orchard Road
Orchard Towers, Orchard Road
Peninsula Shopping Centre, Coleman Street
People's Park Complex, Eu Tong Sen Street
Plaza Singapura, Orchard Road
Shaw Centre, Scotts Road
Specialists' Centre, Orchard Road
Supreme House, Penang Road
Tanglin Shopping Centre, Tanglin Road

Department Stores

Long before World War II, Singapore boasted only two department stores on a grand scale — Robinsons and John Little's. They were stacked with expensive goods from England and America and mostly European residents in Singapore and Malaya shopped there. "Robinsons was where you met friends," one writer recalls. "You could buy baked beans, sausages, Irish stew, even "safe"

Shopping complexes on fashionable Orchard Road. Top, Lucky Plaza; *middle,* Gucci of Italy; *bottom,* Lucky Plaza

47

icecream — all nostalgia of home and England, and evoking thoughts of the next leave." Today it's the Chinese, the Indian, the Moslem, all Singaporeans, who shop in Robinsons and other department stores.

Klasse
Lucky Plaza, Orchard Road

The Metro Group
Metro Golden Mile, Beach Road

Metro Grand
Lucky Plaza, Orchard Road

Mohan Departmental Store
321 Orchard Road

O.G.
Plaza Singapura, Orchard Road

Robinsons
Specialists' Centre, Orchard Road

Yaohan
Plaza Singapura, Orchard Road

Chinese Emporiums

Back in the days before container ships, when junks with bamboo sails came down from China, they had their holds filled with all kinds of exciting wares. They were virtually crocks with Chinese lettering and all tied up with rattan rope. Some were filled with pickled cabbage and others with fish sauce. There were bottles of strong rice wine and Tsingtao beer. Then from wood crates came red lacquer from Beijing, musical instruments from Shanghai and other Chinese ornaments and decorations. All these China-originated wares went into special shops called Chinese Emporiums. The

Indian textile shop on Serangoon Road Rattan and basket weave shop on Arab Street

workmanship was usually not great but the prices couldn't be better. Well, the shops are still there and the only thing that has changed are the prices. Chinese products are more in demand so prices are up. Visit an emporium. It's incredible what they don't carry nowadays.

Chinese
International Building, Orchard Road

Oriental
People's Park Centre, New Bridge Road

Overseas
People's Park Complex, New Bridge Road

Tashing
People's Park Complex, New Bridge Road

Yu Yi
Orchard Building, Grange Road

Singapore has no central shopping area. But there are places where tourists and residents alike favour. **Orchard Road** is to Singapore what the Champs Elysées is to Paris or Fifth Avenue is to New York. On the other hand, **Serangoon Road** is the place to go to buy gold embroidered saris and glittering imitation jewellery. **Raffles Place** is in the downtown business district where you can find good buys in the fine art galleries, mod boutiques and Indian handloom shops. Both **High Street** and **North Bridge Road** are the old arcaded streets that carry everything imaginable. Bargaining here is absolutely essential. **Arab Street** is in a class on its own. Even if you are not interested in shopping it's still a place to go. Take a camera. Singapore's oldest and most interesting shopping mart is **Change Alley**. None are more famous. Leading from Raffles Place to the waterfront, ringing with the noise of shop owners calling out to passing potential customers, you can buy shoes, watches, umbrellas, cutlery and all the gimmick junk from around the world. And here too you can change money, at rates better than the banks offer. The money changers are persistent. There's a story about one Chinese banker who

cut through Change Alley every day for fourteen years, and always the same money changer accosted him with, "Hay, mister, change money?" One day the banker needed to change money and was in a rush, so he stopped for the first time at the money changer. When he got his money he said: "Why, after all these years have you been so persistent when you knew I never stopped?" Without hesitating the money changer said: "You did now." That's Change Alley!

Food, Singapore at Her Best

In Singapore someone doesn't say, "Let's go out and have Chinese food tonight." The Singaporean will specify what food he wants — Cantonese, Szechuan, Teochew. The same with Indian food. He will make a choice, spicy southern Indian, Moslem vegetarian. And for

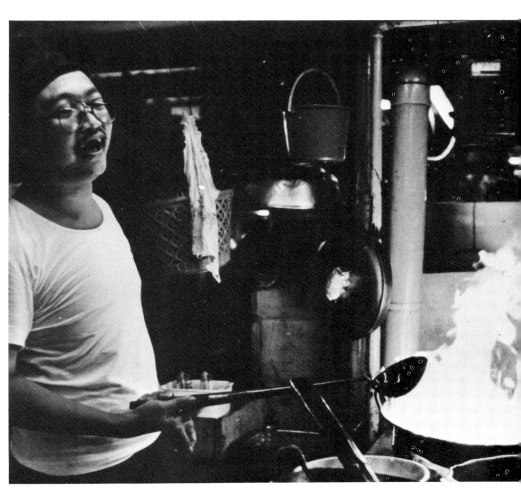

Malay it might include Indonesian, called *Nasi Padang*. And of course, there's *Nonya*, a combination of Malay and Chinese.

What it all boils down to, excuse the pun, is that Singapore's multiculture provides more variety of food than any other city in Southeast Asia, if not all the world. And we haven't even begun to name the types of European food, either French or Italian or Hungarian, nor can we forget the national dishes from other Southeast Asian countries — Japanese, Vietnamese, Thai.

But variety isn't enough to make it great. What gives Singapore food its *tour de force* is it's quality. It's indigenous to the country and people who prepare and serve it. You dine in an Indian restaurant where Indians go to eat; or in a Thai restaurant where the Thais go. Nor can you be fooled by imitation Cantonese food when Cantonese eat there. Chinese *know* their food, as do the Indians, Malays, and the Europeans.

The World of Chinese Food

At one busy night food market they claim to serve 1500 different Chinese dishes. That's what you call variety. In Singapore there's cuisine from every area of China. There's even a Singapore branch called *Nonya* which is fairly hot, resembles Malay food but is adapted to

Money changer working the street in front of Change Alley
The notorious Bugis street is also known for it excellent food

51

Chinese tastes. The main Chinese cuisine you can try is Cantonese, Hokkien, Teochew, Hainanese, Shanghai, Peking, Taiwanese or Szechuan. It would take you years to be a connoisseur of Chinese food. To be more specific, here are a few Singapore specialities: chilli crabs, chilli prawns, fried *meehoon*, Hokkien *mee*, Singapore fried rice, steamboat, sweet-and-sour dishes, Peking duck, Szechuan chicken, Cantonese beef, those luscious tidbits called dim-sum, Chinese pork satay, hundred-year-old eggs, and many, many more.

CANTONESE FOOD

Cathay Restaurant
Cathay Building, Mount Sophia

Eastern Palace
Supreme House, Penang Road

Hilman
Cantonment Road

Majestic Restaurant
Bukit Pasoh Road

Mayflower
DBS Building, Shenton Way

Shang Palace
Shangri-la Hotel, Orange Grove Road

Tropicana
Scotts Road

Dragon Palace
Cockpit Hotel, Oxley Rise

PEKING FOOD

Peking Mayflower Restaurant
International Building, Orchard Road

Pine Court
Mandarin Hotel, Orchard Road

Prima Revolving Restaurant
Keppel Road.

SZECHUAN FOOD

China Palace
Wellington Building, Orchard Road

Chinatown

Tempting bite-size delicacies are a common feature of open air food stalls

Oberoi Imperial Hotel, Jalan Rumbia

Golden Phoenix
Equatorial Hotel, Bukit Timah Road

Hua Palace
Specialists' Centre, Orchard Road

Szechuan Room
Singapura Forum Hotel, Orchard Road

HOKKIEN FOOD

Beng Thin
OCBC Centre, Chulia Street

Prince Room
Selegie Complex, Selegie Road

HUNAN FOOD

San Remo
Orchard Towers, Orchard Road

TEOCHEW FOOD

Swatow Teochew Restaurant
DBS Building, Shenton Way

Tai Seng
Outram Park Complex, Outram Road

Tai Seng Gourmet Corner
Murray Street

HAINANESE FOOD

Chatterbox Coffee House
Mandarin Hotel, Orchard Road

Swee Kee
Middle Road

Yet Con Restaurant
Purvis Street

SHANGHAUNESE FOOD

Great Shanghai
Armenian Street

Other food spots which serve Chinese cuisine are at People's Park in New Bridge Road, Tanjong Pagar Road stalls, The Jalan Sultan Complex, High Street Food Centre at High Street Shopping Centre and of course, the famous stalls in Albert Street and Chinatown.

The World of Indian Food

For those who love highly spiced curry, Singapore offers its best. If you want the spicy goodness of curry without the tears, visit one of the **Kashmir** restaurants. If it's vegetarian dishes you crave then try the **Brahmin** restaurants near Upper Serangoon Road. They serve all you can eat for $1.50, and your plate is a banana leaf. Also cum Indian style, you use your fingers. Some Indian delights to tempt you are chicken, fish and tasty mutton curries, with *chappaties* (flat Indian "bread"); golden *pillau* or beryani rice; *kebabs* on skewers; cold *sambals*; *Tandoori* chicken (Kashmiri); *murtabab* stuffed with meat and onions.

NORTH INDIAN FOOD

Omar Khayam
Hill Street

Rang Mahal
Oberoi Imperial Hotel, Jalan Rumbia

Shalimar
Tanglin Shopping Centre, Tanglin Road

Fresh fruit stand and open air food stalls at Telok Ayer Market in downtown Singapore, popular at lunch time for office workers

Jom Coffee House
Alkaff Building, Market Street

SOUTHERN INDIAN FOOD

Banana Leaf Apollo
Cuff Road

Bilal
International Plaza, Anson Road

Gomez Curry
Selegie House, Selegie Road

Komala Villas
Serangoon Road

The World of Malay Food

If you've never visited this culinary area before, Malay food might be the most intriguing to you. It is different and unusual to the Western palate. Like its close cousin, Indonesian food, it makes tasty use of local ingredients, including coconut milk. *Satay*, a Malay barbecue that's been enthusiastically adopted by all

Singapore races, uses peanuts in its sauce. Local fish cooked the Malay way can be delicious. Don't miss the favourite rice dish, *nasi goreng*. Malay cookery uses all meats but pork, prohibited by Moslem religion. Some Malay foods you'll probably like best are satay, *nasi goreng*, fish and sweet curries. Popular Indonesian food, called *Nasi Padang*, are Javanese curry, famous *rijstaffel*, unusual salads.

MALAY FOOD

Aziza's Restaurant
36 Emerald Hill Road

Rendezvous Restaurant
Bras Basah Road

Indonesian Cafe Restaurant
Apollo Hotel

For Indonesian rijstaffel:
Siamese Seafood Restaurant
Cockpit Hotel. (lunchtime Saturdays,
Sundays)

NONYA FOOD

Luna Coffee House
Apollo Hotel, Havelock Road

Other Foods of Asia

JAPANESE FOOD
Japanese food, sometimes, served while
you sit on *tatami*, is available at:

Fujiya
Shenton House, Shenton Way

Hoshigaoka Saryp
Apollo Hotel, Havelock Road

Left, *one of the many sliced fresh fruit
stands found around Singapore;* centre
*Indian stall on North Bridge Road; local
pastry,* above

Kampachi
Hotel Equatorial, Bukit Timah Road

Kanako
Goodwood Park Hotel, Scotts Road

Yamagen
Yen Sen Building, Orchard Road

Yamoto
Wisma Indonesia, Orchard Road

KOREAN FOOD

Han Do
Orchard Shopping Centre, Orchard
Road

Korean Restaurant
Specialists' Centre, Orchard Road

THAI FOOD

Siamese Seafood Restaurant
Cockpit Hotel, Oxley Rise

The World of Western Food

For anyone who wants Western food
there's no shortage in Singapore. There
are many fine restaurants. You can
choose a MacDonald's hamburger stand
— and it's become very popular in
Singapore — or some first class
Continental style establishments. For
example, **Hugo's** in the Hyatt Hotel has
been acclaimed as the finest Continental
restaurant in Asia. Most first class
restaurants now buy their prime steaks
and even their vegetables abroad. Waiters
are European trained. The atmosphere
can be very sophisticated, or it can be
very "pubby." Some of the more popular
Western restaurants are listed here:

AMERICAN

Copper Kettle
Shaw Centre, Scotts Road

Kentucky Fried Chicken
Orchard Road

MacDonald's
Liat Towers, Orchard Road

*Kentucky Fried Chicken in the Lucky
Plaza on Orchard Road*

AUSTRIAN

Cafe Vienna
Holiday Inn, Scotts Road

De Viennese
Specialists' Centre, Orchard Road

FRENCH

Belvedere
Mandarin Hotel, Orchard Road

La Chaumiere Cafe and Restaurant
Orchard Road

ENGLISH

The Beefeater
River Valley Road

Fosters
Amber Mansions, Orchard Road

Jockey
Shaw Centre, Scotts Road

Stables
Mandarin Hotel, Orchard Road

La Rotonde Brasserie
Hotel Marco Polo, Tanglin Road

Le Grill
Ming Court Hotel, Tanglin Road

GERMAN

Baron's Table
Holiday Inn, Scotts Road

Grunewald Chicken Grill
International Plaza, Anson Road

ITALIAN

Jack's Place
Killiney Road

La Taverna
Emerald Hill Road

Palm Court
Raffles Hotel, Beach Road

Pete's Place
Hyatt Hotel, Scotts Road

MEXICAN

Country Club Hotel
Upper East Coast Road

De Viennese
Specialists' Centre, Orchard Road

RUSSIAN

Troika
DBS Building, Shenton Way

SCOTTISH

Gordon Grill

Goodwood Park Hotel, Scotts Road

SPANISH

Emperors' Room
Hotel Royal-Ramada, Newton Road

SWISS

Chesa
Hotel Equatorial, Bukit Timah Road

Le Chalet
Ladyhill Hotel, Ladyhill Road

CONTINENTAL

Cairnhill Steak House
Cairnhill Road

Golden Peacock
Shangri-la Hotel, Orange Grove Road

Harbour Grill
Singapore Hilton, Orchard Road

Hugo's Hyatt Hotel
Scotts Road.

Dining Out Cheaply

There are literally hundreds of hawkers stalls, or "fast food centres" as they are now called, dotted all over the island. In fact there is hardly a street corner where you won't find one. They are all good and inexpensive. Prices are listed on all stalls. The more popular and accessible for the visitors are as follows:

Buffet at the Hilton Hotel on Orchard Road

Empress Place Food Centre on the river front next to the Immigration Department is well patronised by the locals and usually quite crowded. You can dine and have a view of the boat traffic on the river.

Glutton's Corner, downtown on **Anson Road**, has a good selection of Indian and Malay food in addition to the Chinese.

Newton Circus stalls are at the junction of **Bukit Timah Road, Scotts Road** and **Clemenceau Avenue**. It's one of the biggest and certainly most popular in Singapore at night. It has a wide selection of Chinese, Indian and Nonya dishes.

Telok Ayer Market on **Shenton Way**. This is a huge Victorian octagonal building packed full of eating stalls. It

For those with an adventurous palate Singapore's food centres offer many delights

gets very crowded at 1 pm., when the local office workers have lunch. Most of the stalls are closed at night.

The Satay Club is down on **Queen Elizabeth Walk** at the sea front. As the name says, satay is the speciality. Chilli crab is also on the menu.

Rasa Singapura Food Centre is small, with only 24 tables, but it is quite attractive (with lots of plants around). It's located behind the Handicraft Centre in Tanglin Road. The STPB claims it has the best hawker stall food in Singapore. Other areas might disagree.

Cuppage Road Food Centre at Cuppage Road, off **Orchard Road**, is where some of the renowned "Car Park" food stalls across from Cold Storage Supermarket have been re-located. These stalls and others are now in a ventilated buildings

instead of being in the open air.

Sports

When asked by the press why on earth he came to Singapore in 1922 to run a rubber plantation, a retiring British planter remarked: "Because when Dunlop hired me they were forming a rugby team." The reporter thought the Englishmen was jesting, but, of course, he was not. "Where else could I play rugby 12 months out of the year!" the Englishman added. It was true, the British came to work, but they also brought their sports with them. Many have survived to this day. Cricket matches are played on the **Padang** every weekend, polo twice a week at **Thompson Road**, and every school has its rugby team. Bright skies and warm weather in Singapore make it a sportsman's paradise, as the British discovered. Literally dozens of sports clubs and associations are dedicated to sporting games and health improvement. The main sports centres are the **National Stadium**, the **Jalan Besar Stadium**, the **Singapore Badminton Hall**, and the **Farrer Park Athletic Centre**. In recent years posh private clubs for health improvement and weight reducing have become fashionable in Singapore. **Tropamara** in the UIC Building on Shenton Way is the newest and most grandiose one in town. The Mandarin and Hilton Hotels, and several other first class hotels, also have super health clubs with sauna baths and jacuzzis. For more information on sporting activities, contact the **Singapore Sports Council**, tel: 446-7111.

Badminton has always been popular in Singapore but it has reached new heights in recent years with the relaxed relationship with mainland China. Chinese teams are always coming to Singapore to compete. **Singapore**

Girl's Cricket Team on the Padang

Badminton Hall on **Gullemard Road** is the place to go if you want to play. Courts are available for use from 7 am to 11 pm. Bookings must be made before noon. Fees are $2-3 per hour. Tel: 245-122

Bowling is another Singapore pastime well enjoyed. Most alleys open at 10 am and close at 1:00 am. Charges average $1.80.
Jackies Bowl (Katong), 542-B East Coast Road. Tel: 416-519
Jackies Bowl (Orchard), 8 Grange Road. Tel: 374-744
Jurong Family Bowl, Yuan Ching Road. Tel: 655-433
Kallang Bowl, Leisure Drome, Kallang Park. Tel: 446-0545
Pasir Panjang Bowl, 9.5 km., Pasir Panjang Road. Tel: 775-5555
Plaza Bowl, 7th floor, Textile Centre, Jalan Sultan. Tel: 292-4821
Starbowl, 5th floor, Peach Centre, Sophia Road. Tel: 31-421

Cricket Club was first opened in 1832. Cricket has been popular ever since. The club house is on the Esplanade. Tel: 39-271

Cycling in Singapore is popular but not for tourists, except on Sentosa Island, where you can rent bicycles by the hour or by the day.

Flying. Republic of Singapore Flying Club is the oldest in Southeast Asia. It's located at Building 140-b, **Seletar Airbase.** Tel: 481-0200. You can rent a plane or take instructions.

Golf is Singapore's social game played by many businessmen, including the Prime Minister. The major courses are: **Changi Golf Club**, Netheravon Road. Tel: 545-1298. Charges: $20 per game; $3 for golf clubs, $4 caddy fee. Non-members, weekdays only. **Jurong Country Club**, Science Centre Road. Tel: 655-655 Charges: $40 per game; $15 for golf club, $6-8 caddy fee. Non-members,

weekdays only. **Parklane Golf Driving Range**, East Coast Park. Tel: 440-6726 Charges: $1.25 for 50 balls before 3.30 pm.; $1.75 for 50 balls after 3.30 pm. Open from 7 am. to 11 pm. **Sembawang Country Club**, 17 km., Sembawang Road. Tel: 257-4714 Charges: $30 per game on weekdays; $40 on weekends; $15 for golf clubs; $7 caddy fee. **Sentosa Golf Club**, Sentosa Tel: 622-722. Charges: $30 whole day weekdays: $60 per game on weekends; $15 for golf clubs; $7 caddy fee. **Singapore Island Country Club**, Upper Thompson Road. Tel: 453-1222 Charges: $70 per game, $15 for golf clubs, $10 caddy fee; $3 for shoes. Non-members, weekdays only. **Tanglin Golf Course**, Minden Road. Tel: 637-236. Charges: $5 per game on weekdays; $7 on weekends, $3 for golf clubs; 50 cents for caddy carts. **The Keppel Club**, Bukit Chermin Road. Tel: 272-9305. Charges: $30 per game on weekdays only; $10 for golf clubs; $7 caddy fee.

Horse Racing. Singapore Turf Club, Bukit Timah Road. Tel: 468-3366. There are seven race meetings of four days' racing each in a year, and two additional two-day amateur meetings. For race dates, check the local papers. Admission $2.

Jogging. At the Padang in the cool of morning it's time to join the joggers. If you care to run with an outrageous group of runners, join the **Hash House Harriers** on Monday night. Visitors are invited. But be prepared for some rough mud-soaked terrain, however, the beer bash that follows is well worth it.

Polo. Singapore Polo Club, Thompson Road. Tel: 253-5548. Polo is on Tuesday, Thursday, Saturdays and Sundays from 5.30 pm (except from November to January). Spectators are welcome.

Scuba Diving. The **Singapore Sub-Aqua Club** is located at 41 Sixth Avenue, Off

Dunearn Road, Tel: 486-0944. The
Aquamarine Club, 1404 Shaw Towers,
Beach Road, organizes weekend diving
trips and longer trips once each month to
various reefs in Southeast Asia. Tel: 293-
4212. Another active club is **Dive
Masters**, 27 Lorong Tukang Satu. Tel:
650-658.

Squash and Tennis. Squash has taken off
in Singapore in the last few years. There
are courts galore. Listed here are both
squash and tennis courts. Charges from
$2-5 depending on time of day.

Alexandra Park, Royal Road, off York
and Bedford Road. Tel: 637-236.
Changi Squash and Tennis Courts,
Cranwell Road. Tel: 445-2941. **Farrer
Park**, Rutland Road. Tel: 514-166.
National Stadium, Kallang. Tel: 245-
1222. **Seletar Squash and Tennis Courts**,
3 Park Lane, SAF Seletar Base Tel: 481-
4745. **Singapore Squash and Tennis
Courts Centre**, Fort Canning Rise,
Central Park. Tel: 360-155. **Water Skiing**.
Ponggol Boatel, Ponggol Point. Tel: 882-
788. Charges: $40 per hour of ski boat
with ski equipment.

Festivals

If you can imagine a multi-racial society
with Chinese, Malays, Indians,
Indonesian and Europeans, and all of
them keen on celebrating their own
cultural and religious holidays, you know
then there's certain to be endless
festivities throughout the year. Singapore
could easily be called The City of
Festivals. In the list of festivals below,
European holidays are not included.
Since most Eastern festivals are based on
the months by moons, check for dates in
the Western calender.

Chinese New Year
This is a festive occasion for the Chinese
but not for the tourist who arrives looking
for shopping bargains. Shops and
department stores are closed three or four
days. But nevertheless, Chinese New
Year is colourful. Come New Year's Eve

and you will see red scrolls with verses on them pasted in newly spruced homes. Red banners are hung over doors. All this in the hope that the evil spirits will be driven away.

Chinese cakes, waxed ducks and Mandarin oranges are a must for all Chinese homes. A re-union dinner takes place on New Year's Eve, and for the first three days of the year the streets are quiet.

And on Chinese New Year itself, all Singaporeans greet each other with "Kong Hee Fatt Choy" (a wish for prosperity and happiness). *Angpows* — red envelopes with money inside — are given to children and elders. Singapore's streets are filled with people bedecked in new clothes. Visiting relatives and paying respects is the order of the day.

Chingay

The Chingay parade is an annual burst of colour and music — cymbals, drums and Chinese bands fill the Singapore air with raucous notes as floats, pugilistic shows and lion dances entertain the people along the routes of the parade. A must for every tourist who is in Singapore.

Thaipusam

This has to be one of the most unusual, bizarre religious rites seen in Southeast Asia today. Thaipusam underlines man's capacity to have the mind prevail over matter, or in this case, over pain. The festival is in honour of Hindu deity Lord Subramaniom. Devotees do penance by carrying *kavadis* from the **Perumal Temple** in Serangoon Road to the **Chettiar Temple** at **Tank Road**. *Kavadis* are decorations, often fan-shaped, made from steel. The bottom of each *kavadi* has sharp steel points which pierce carrier's bare body and thus help support the weight. Other devotees may drive spikes and skewers through their tongue or cheeks. But the carrier feels no pain

Lion dances and youth parades are features at the National Day Celebrations

and there is no blood. It has to be seen to be believed. Hundreds of devotees and their followers lead an all-day procession. Shouts of "vel! vel!" and the beat of drums fill the air. This, certainly, is the mysterious Orient.

Songkran Festival
This is a Buddhist celebration, known also as "The Thai Water Festival". The New Year is ushered in by Buddhist bathing the statute of Buddha. There are two temples where this unusual festival can be seen, the **Anada Metyarana Temple** (Silat Road) and the **Sattha Puchaniyaram Temple** (Holland Road).

Vesak Day
Another Buddhist event. The celebration is in honour of Buddha, the founder of this religion. Devoted Buddhists feed the poor on this day and refrain from eating meat. Saffron robed Buddhist monks chant verses throughout the day at the **Temple of One Thousand Lights**. Take a tape recorder as well as a camera.

Hari Raya Puasa
This is the Moslem New Year. It marks the end of Ramadan — the 30-day fasting period for Moslems. There are prayers at mosques and friends and relatives visit each other. It is only exciting for visitors, however, if they have Moslem friends.

Dragon Boat
The Dragon Boat Festival has both history behind it and a lot of sporty action to watch. (The problem is finding an ideal location to watch the action. The best way is to rent a sampan.) Teams of athletic enthusiasts in long, sleek-lined boats (shaped like dragons with a head and tail at opposite ends) compete through a series of racing heats, requiring great synchronisation of group rowing skills. A drummer, atop a mounted

Hindu youth at thaipusan Festival doing penance

platform amidship, beats out an uncanny rythmn on a huge drum to urge on the rowers to the finish-line.

The old story: It's thought that a Chinese statesman's death by drowning in 290 BC started the whole thing. Disillusioned with the corruption of the Imperial Court in which he served, Chu Yuan threw himself into the sea to protest the indifference of his emperor. In an effort to recover his body, the people of Hunan, China, set out in row-boats, casting overboard glutinous rice cakes wrapped in bamboo leaves and splashing their oars about in the water to distract the fish nearby. In any event, the rice dumplings remain a big part of the festival, not thrown at fishes, but mainly gobbled up during the festival by racers and onlookers alike. Competing teams come from all around Asia; there are also local contests.

Birthday of the Monkey God
This colourful festival in honour of the Monkey God (T'se Tien Tai Seng Yeh) is celebrated lavishly twice a year in several

Chinese temples.

This is the Chinese version of Thaipusam, almost. Mediums with skewers pierced through their cheeks and tongues go into a trance during the ceremony and write out special charms with their blood. *Wayang* (Chinese street opera) and puppet shows are performed in the temple courtyard. Processions are held at the temples on **Eng Hoon Street** and **Cumming Street**. Many Chinese parents ask the Monkey God to be godfather of their children so they might grow up as tough and hardy as him. The Monkey God is also believed to cure the sick.

Birthday of the Saint of the Poor

This is a festival surely to awe tourists. The image of the Saint (Kong Teck Choon Ong) is carried in a brightly decorated palanquin by Chinese worshippers and accompanied by spirit mediums with their arms, cheeks and tongues pierced with skewers.

The entire procession starts from **White Cloud Temple** on **Granges Avenue**, tours the neighbourhood and returns to the temple. As the chair passes the crowds on the streets, young and old press their hands together in reverence.

Birthday of the Third Prince

The Third Prince of the Lotus, a child god, is worshipped as a hero and miracle-worker. He holds a magic bracelet in one hand, a magic spear in the other and rides on "wind and fire" wheels. During the celebrations, mediums demonstrate their powers by lashing themselves with swords and spiked maces. A Taoist temple dedicated to the Third Prince is near the junction of **Clarke Street** and **North Boat Quay**. A street procession takes place here in the afternoon.

Left *Monkey God at Chinese Temple*
Right, *National Day celebrations*

71

National Day
This is the most celebrated and colourful day of the year. It's a proud and truly multi-racial occasion as Singapore celebrates her emergence (since 1965) as an independent republic. There are performances by military bands, girl bagpipers, pugilists and acrobats, cultural dance displays, lion and dragon dances. In the evening, a gigantic fireworks display lights up the sky in many parts of the city.

Ramadan
All Moslems are required to observe daylight fasting for one month. Special prayers are held in mosques every evening. The scene behind **Sultan Mosque** on **North Bridge Road** near Arab Street is a colourful one. Dozens of stalls sell all kinds of Malay cakes and Indian food in anticipation of the breaking of the fast at about 6:30 pm. every evening.

Festival of the Hungry Ghosts
The Chinese believe that during the seventh month, the souls of the dead are released from purgatory to roam the earth. Joss sticks are burnt in every home; prayers, food and "ghost money" are offered to appease the ghosts. Market stallholders combine to hold massive celebrations to ensure that their business will prosper in the coming year. *Wayang* (Chinese street opera) and puppet shows are performed during the festival and loads of fruit and Chinese delicacies are offered to the spirits of the dead.

Moon Cake Festival
The Chinese love to eat, as we see in this festival. According to the Chinese, the moon is at its roundest and brightest on the fifteenth night of the eight moon. On this night, they celebrate by eating moon cakes. One legend says that in ancient China, secret messages of revolt were smuggled to the people in moon cakes

Left, *after the parade on National Day*
Right, *worshipers at Hindu temple on Serangoon Road*

and led to the overthrow of the tyrannical Mongol dynasty. Moon cakes are filled with a mixture of bean paste and lotus seeds and sometimes a duck egg. They may not sound tasty but actually they are. Shops in Chinatown are filled with colourful paper lanterns in the shape of airplanes and animals. On the night of the festival, children light their lanterns while housewives burn joss sticks and candles and offer moon cakes, pomelos, yams and prayers to the full moon.

Festival of the Nine Emperor Gods

The Chinese say that the Nine Emperor Gods cure ailments and bring luck, wealth and longevity. From the first day to the ninth day of the ninth moon the Nine Emperor Gods are worshipped and many people become vegetarian for a time as an expression of penitence. *Wayang* (Chinese street opera) and colourfully decorated floats enliven the proceedings. In the evening, the images of the Nine Emperor Gods are paraded on decorated sedan chairs to the accompaniment of cymbals and drums and followed by throngs of people bearing yellow flags and banners to the sea. The two main temples are at **8 km. Upper Serangoon Road** and at **Lorong Tai Seng**.

Pilgrimage to Kusu Island

Try not to miss this festival, and prepare to get splashed. During the month-long festival, 100,000 Taoist pay their annual respects to Tua Pek Kong, the God of Prosperity, on **Kusu Island** 6.5 km. to the south. To join them, take the ferry that leaves **Clifford Pier** at hourly intervals from 6:30 am. to 6:30 pm. daily. Roundtrip $3. Children $1.50. Pilgrims take with them offerings of chicken, pink-shelled eggs, fruit, flowers, joss sticks and candles. They pray for prosperity, good health and obedient children. Both Chinese and Malays visit Kusu Island. Legend has it that two shipwreck survivors, a Chinese and a Malay, were marooned on Kusu Island and lived there harmoniously till their death. Now the island houses the **Tua Pek Kong Temple** at one end and the shrine of a Malay saint at the other.

Thimithi (Fire Walking) Festival

You have to see it to believe it. The Hindus celebrate this festival to honour greatness and purity of goddess Droba-Devl. At 3 pm., a procession starts from the **Perumai Temple** on **Serangoon Road** and passes through Selegie Road, Prinsep Street, Bras Basah Road and North Bridge Road, ending at the **Mariamman**

Temple on **South Bridge Road**. At 4 pm., devotees in a trance walk over a pit of burning charcoal to fulfil their vows. Don't try it. The coals are hot.

Deepavali
This is the Hindu festival of lights. There are a number of legends as to its origin. It signifies the victory of good over evil. It is the Hindu New Year and merriment is the order of the day. Hindus light up their houses at night with candles or oil lamps. It can be fun if you have Hindu friends.

Prophet Mohammed's Birthday
It is best to see the celebration of Prophet Mohammed's Birthday at the **Sultan Mosque**, near **Arab Street**. On this day,

Moslems have long prayer sessions. Hymns are chanted and the life of Prophet Mohammed is recited.

Children, left, *and Lion dancers,* right, *at the National Day celebrations*

Passport to Adventure
— Off The Beaten Track

Singapore has been labelled a "shopper's paradise," and it's difficult to convince visitors the republic has anything else to offer. The average visitor spends less than three days in Singapore, and most of that time is taken up with shopping. Stand at **Clifford Pier** and watch the passengers — Russians, Poles, Scandinavians, Italians, Greeks, Koreans, Indonesians, Australians — watch them all disembark from liners and cruise ships anchored in the roads. They step ashore wide-eyed, a bit sceptical and uncertain at first, and in a few hours they are back, smiling and chattering, arms laden with packages and boxes and plastic carrying bags bulging with instant cameras and electrical appliances and all imaginable kinds of souvenirs and gadgetry. They leave Singapore much contented, but are none the wiser.

Singapore is more than shopping. There is a great deal to see and discover.

The harbour is one of the most exciting in the world, yet very few people, residents included, ever get to see or know it. Singapore and its many islands are ringed with reefs where you can see magnificant living coral and myriads of tropical fish, or where you can hunt for treasures. Yes, real treasure! There are *kelongs*, or fishing houses, built on stilts out at sea, and it's possible to visit one at night when the fisherman have their nets lowered and bring in bountiful catches. But you needn't go that far. There's Singapore Island, even Singapore City. Who has ever walked the entire length of the Singapore River, or explored the back alleys of Chinatown by foot? Or hired a car and driven into the Singapore countryside through farms and *copra* plantations to far-removed coves along the **Straits of Johore**? It's all there, for anyone who wants to go looking for adventure.

Chinatown by Foot

A tour of **Chinatown** can hardly be called
"off-the-beaten path" but on the other
hand, what you seldom see are tourists
who do it alone by foot. It's the most
exciting way to see Chinatown. Take
along a good map, or better yet the
Singapore Guide and Street Directory,
and a good pair of walking shoes. Don't
be afraid to get lost, for after all, that
might be part of the adventure. A good
place to start a tour of Chinatown is at
Raffles Place in the centre of town. Turn
north on **Malacca Street** and you arrive
at **Telok Ayer Street**. Until 1845 Telok
Ayer was the waterfront. Then came
Singapore's first reclamation and today
the street is a 400 metres from the
sea. Some of the original buildings still
stand. Shophouses are two and three
storey, with bars on the windows and
grated doors at street level. The
architecture here is Chinese baroque,
brought from Europe and mixed with
Chinese styles. There are balconies and
overhangs. Above the eaves and arches
far above the street, moss grows on the
walls and in places vines are rooted into
the brick fabric and cracks. Don't
hesitate to venture up any of the side
streets. At **Pekin** you can have a quick
lunch at a local food stall, at **Cross Street**
you can pick up gold jewellery and at
Boon Tat you can visit a Moslem Tamil
Temple.

Leave **Telok Ayer Street** at Amoy and
turn right. Amoy is a street of association
halls and clan houses, all with brightly
painted banners hanging outside. The
buildings are among some of the oldest in
Singapore. Heavy wooden beams and
supporting arches are bent with age.
Tailor and barber shops and dentist's
office are unlike any you'd find on
Orchard Road. Amoy swings back to
Cross Street where you make a left turn,
and another left at **Club Street**. The
avenue begins an upward climb and is a
reminder of Grant Street in San
Francisco. Or is Grant Street like
Singapore's Club Street?

Club Street is quiet for Chinatown.

Deep in darkened doorways, old women sit playing *mahjong*. In woodcarving shops craftsmen are bent over their works of religious motifs. And if you want a shave, a barber has a chair set up on the street under the cool arcade.

Follow Club Street around to the right and you will see one of Singapore's most unusual professions, curbside letter writers.

Exploring the Singapore River

A walking trip few people ever make is the length of the **Singapore River**. The five kilometre river cuts through the very heart of the city.

For its size it's probably one of the most important and busiest rivers in the world. It's possible to follow it from its mouth at **Anderson Street Bridge** to its very source near **River Valley Road**. The amount of traffic carried upon this small river is incredible. A photographer can find many worthwhile scenes.

At times it may be necessary to cross from one side to the other. It's best to begin at the bridge and work your way up river as far as you can go. At the lower end of the river there are **Hallpike's Boatyard**, some very old godowns and Singapore's very first ice house. The full history of these and other landmarks are listed in the *Singapore Guide and Street Directory*.

Beyond the **Clemenceau Avenue Bridge** the walk leads to **Robertson Quay**. If you want to follow the river to its limits don't cross the bridge but continue up the left bank to where **Alexander Canal** and Singapore River become one.

Exploring Singapore Island

Whoever would imagine making a trip to Singapore to see a rubber plantation, visit a Malay village, or trek through the jungles?

Well, you can. The rural side of Singapore is one that few people know, or

Cobbler on Waterloo Street; centre, *a potter at Handicraft Centre and trishaw driver with customer;* bottom, *wood carver at Handicraft Centre*

even imagine exists.

Visitors are always surprised to discover there's more to Singapore than godowns and customs sheds, high-rises and housing flats and a pulsating commercial port. Singapore island can boast of miles of beaches, rubber estates and farms, Malay *kampongs* and forest reserves with their original primary jungles.

Singapore shares with Rio de Janeiro the distinction of being a major tropical city with an area of rain forest in its midst. In the very middle of Singapore is **Bukit** (*Hill*) **Timah**. It rises to 177 metres and is surrounded by 3,200 hectares of original rain forest. It was made into a reserve in 1833.

Adjacent to the Bukit Timah Reserve is a water catchment with secondary forest and three artificial lakes. The Reserve and the Water Catchment are

Looking northward along the Singapore River
Left, *Botanical Gardens and* over, *a* kelong *in the Straits*

the core of Singapore's present wildlife population. Singapore Island has some 30 known land animals and 16 species of bats, or about one third of the total mammals of the Malay Peninsula, which is nearly 400 times larger.

Within the last few years the *Straits Times* has reported a panther on the loose and on several occasions the newspaper carried stories about 5 and 6 metre long pythons being seen on golf courses and crossing highways. In 1979 a 4 metre crocodile made headlines when it was seen in the **Kallang River**. A climb to the top of **Bukit Timah** will give the visitor a first-hand view of the forest that once covered the entire island. Bukit Timah can be reached by bus or taxi, but to explore rural Singapore a car is essential, along with a good road map. You can rent a car from **Avis** or any number of car rental agencies.

A good example of rural Singapore is to take a drive to **Tampines** on the northeast side of the island. A long quiet road leads to the area. There is little traffic. Small rubber holdings and farms

are often hidden from view by dense shrubs and trees.

Chinese farmers and their families work ceaselessly throughout the day, tending their vegetable plots and feeding their pigs and chickens. Some of the side roads are so small and winding that even road maps are of little help.

A booming business in rural Singapore is raising orchids. In 1979 alone, exports of cut roses earned $8.4 million.

Along Singapore's **West Coast Road** is **Sungai Pandan**, or **Pandan River**. It's a port of entry for trading boats from Indonesia. The river is a total contrast to the busy harbour a few miles away, where supertankers and containerships from the world over come to rest. Here at **Sungai Pandan**, Rhio trading boats without engines kedge their way up the river by working two anchors.

Their cargoes are not transistors from Japan or oil from the Middle East, but bundles of rattan from Sumatra, firewood from Java, charcoal from Banka and raw salt from Burma. Here, along the stone jetty, it's manpower and not heavy cranes that does the loading and unloading.

Malay *kampongs* are fewer than they were several years ago, but nevertheless they do exist. *Kampong* houses, built on stilts and with high vaulting ceilings, date back hundreds of years. The Malays take great pride in their villages and mosques. Every village, no matter how small, will have its prayer house.

Branching out from downtown Singapore, there's both an East Coast and West Coast Road. Reclamation has moved the sea farther away and rich Regency style Chinese mansions no longer have a view but many still stand in all their splendour. Unfortunately their days are numbered.

Visiting a *Kelong*

When your jet begins to drop low and make its final approach to Singapore, you will notice dozens of small *attap* shacks, built high on stilts, jutting far out to sea. Some appear to be miles from land, while others hug the coast and jam the narrow straits between Singapore Island and **Johore**.

If you wonder what they are, or why they are there, don't feel left out. The same question puzzled Raffles, the founder of Singapore, when he first made the scene in 1819. An officer aboard ship made reference to them, stating that the land certainly had to be hostile, since the local inhabitants lived in houses at sea. These *attap* houses, they soon discovered, were called *kelongs*, and they were not actually permanent dwelling places but seagoing fishing sheds.

Times in Singapore have changed the skyline from jungle to godown and finally to super concrete and glass sky-scrapers, but the silhouette and function of the *kelongs* have not changed since Raffles' day.

A truly interesting experience is a visit to a *kelong*, and preferably at night, when all the activity takes place. The only problem is getting there. Singapore encourages tourists in other directions. One of the reasons for their concern is fear of fire. Understandably then, *kelongs* are not on the list of "musts" of the government tourist board. But visiting one is still possible. If you don't have a Chinese friend who can arrange it, contact the bumboats for hire at **Clifford Pier**. Explain what you want and chances are the boatman will oblige. Time was when a *kelong* was off-limits to women. A Singaporean might still tell you that the opposite sex is not permitted on a *kelong,* but I haven't seen any that enforce the ruling. Supposedly, women brought bad luck.

Have your boatman take you before dark. It's a good idea to carry drinking water, something to nibble on and a blanket. Usually about three in the morning, between hauling in the nets, a cat nap will help. And *kelongs* do get cold. A *kelong*, primitive as it may appear, is a remarkable piece of architecture. Built on stilts that may extend 3 metres in the mud and project 9 to 12 metres from the floor of the ocean to the surface, they are constructed to

withstand changing currents, high winds and raging seas. And there's not a nail or metal clamp holding them together.

Not any one can build a *kelong*. In Singapore a licence must be obtained from the government, and there are strict regulations concerning where and how they are to be built. The major concern is that they do not become hazardous to shipping. It's not unusual for a team to spend six months on the construction of a kelong, at a cost of more than $20,000. It's a great price to pay considering kelongs seldom last 10 years. At five years they begin to need major repairs.

You may not get much sleep, and you may return with heartburn from the chilli crab (sometimes fishermen cook them up at night), but a kelong trip is one you are certain to enjoy. It will have to be unorganised, and the only costs will be your transportation there and back. For the shutter-bug there are great opportunities for some original photos, especially sunset and early dawn shots. At night, of course, a flash would be needed.

Fishermen pulling in their net on Singapore's eastern shore

Travellers Tips

Singapore Tourist Promotion Board

The red logo of a "merlion", a lion's head with the body of a mermaid, is the Singapore Tourist Promotion Board's stamp of approval. And in a country where tourism is big business and a major dollar earner, the STPB, a statutory body of the Singapore Government, wields indisputable power. A few years ago tourists complained about the many shops advertising as "duty-free" shops, which actually they were not. In one sweep of law's arm, "duty-free" signs came down. Today the only shop authorised to advertise "duty-free" is one at the airport.

You will find the STPB office and information desks helpful if you need specific information or free brochures and maps. Also if you want the service of an official tourist guide, receptionists can make the arrangements. A guide costs $18 for the first three hours. The main office located at **131 Tudor Court, Tanglin Court, Tanglin Road** is open from 8 am. to 5 pm. daily except Sundays and public holidays. Telephone: 235-6616. STPB maintains a second Information Counter at the Airport Arrival Hall, open from 6 am. to 10 pm. daily.

Open air diners at Albert Street, one of Singapore's favourite eateries

Visa Requirements

If any country deserves credit for its efficient customs and immigration service, the Singapore government does, considering that each year 43,000 ships arrive, over five and a half million passengers use **Paya Lebar Airport** and more than two million tourists descend upon this tiny republic. Few places in the world have entrance requirements as lenient as Singapore's. Visitors can remain up to three months, other than for employment.

U.K. and Commonwealth passport holders, U.S. and West European (non-Communist) nationals do not require visas for Singapore. Nationals of most other non-Communist countries with confirmed onward reservations can transit for 14 days without a visa. Identity card holders from Hong Kong or Taiwan require a visa.

Vaccinations

Cholera, yellow fever and smallpox certificates are required if the traveller has been in infected areas within five, six or 14 days respectively, of his or her arrival in Singapore. All visitors from **Somalia** and **Ethiopia** must have valid smallpox and yellow fever certificates.

Customs

Customs clearance is very simple and quite speedy in Singapore. Besides your personal things, you can take in duty-free gifts up to a reasonable value, also duty free are 200 cigarettes, one bottle of liquor, and one of wine. Prohibited items include firearms, explosives, narcotics and pornographic material. There is an airport tax of $15 when you depart, so don't change all your money. Flights to Malaysia are taxed $6.

Medical Services

Don't get sick in Singapore! Singapore has no free health service and becoming ill can prove to be more expensive than back home, unless you are well covered with medical insurance. Medical facilities in Singapore are good. Most major hotels have their own staff doctors on a 24-hour call and a visit will cost you about $60. Other doctors are listed under "Medical Practitioners" in the Yellow Pages of the *Singapore Phone Book*. Dentists are listed under "Dental Surgeons." In case of a road accident or other emergencies, an ambulance will answer a 999 telephone call and take you to the nearest Government Hospital. You cannot be taken to a private one, but you can transfer later. Costs in private hospitals average from $65 for a three-bed ward to $130 for a single bedroom with bath. Two private hospitals are:

Gleaneagles Hospital
Napier Road,
Tel: 637-222

Mount Alvernia Hospital
Thompson Road,
Tel: 538-844

Singapore has 13 government hospitals which cost $60 a day for first class. The four major Government Hospitals are listed below:

Alexandra Hospital
Alexandra Road,
Tel: 635-222

Singapore General Hospital
Outram Road,
Tel: 222-3322

Tan Tock Seng Hospital
Moulmain Road,
Tel: 256-6011

Toa Payoh Hospital
Tao Payoh Raise,
Tel: 256-0411

Climate and Clothing

Joseph Conrad wrote about the "suffocating heat" and Somerset Maugham thought the monsoons "were maddening," and no wonder. The women characters in their novels wore high-neck brocaded dresses and long white gloves, while the men sported bush jackets and solar *topees* by day and formal dinner jackets by night. Nor did they have air-

conditioned taxis to drive to air-conditioned Robinsons Department Store to do their shopping. And there were no air-conditioned cocktail lounges to gather with friends and drink tall iced drinks. In fact, there wasn't even ice. In Singapore today, where it's a $500 fine to throw a cigarette end on the street and water directly from the tap is the safest in the world, it's hard to imagine that a hundred year ago people in Singapore died from malaria and plague and had to fear tigers in the night. It certainly isn't that way today.

Although Singapore is less than 130 kilometres from the Equator, it has a surprisingly mild climate. The only precautions visitors should take is to stay out of the sun for long periods. The average daytime temperature is 29C°., and the average at night is 23.8C°. With Singapore now almost completely air-conditioned no-one even bothers about the heat.

The heaviest rainfalls occur between November and January, but rain is usual throughout the year. A monsoon rain will last but a few hours at the most. Your wardrobe should be selected accordingly. Evening wear runs to jackets and ties in fashionable air-conditioned places.

Transportation

Singapore island is crisscrossed by excellent roads and there is a new highways system that skirts the southern fringe of the island, crossing rivers and harbours, and offers an exciting panoramic view of the city on one side and on the other the vast harbour with hundreds of ships at anchor and the islands of Indonesia beyond.

Getting around in Singapore is not difficult; it's just a matter of choice on how you want to get there and how much you can afford to pay. You can travel by bus, taxi, hired car, coach, ferry, junk, sampan, motor launch, helicopter, private plane, railway, cable car or trishaw. You can step aboard a ferry in Singapore at **Clifford Pier** and voyage to Sentosa Island, or travel there by cable car. You can take a bus, taxi, private car or trishaw to the railway station and journey

Old shop houses along Tanglin Road

by train across the island to **Johore,** or remain aboard and travel 2,400 kilometres northward through dense rubber plantations and tropical jungles to Bangkok, a two and a half day journey away.

The rule of the road when travelling in Singapore is to keep to the left and the vehicle on the right has the right-of-way. Jaywalking is strictly prohibited and heavy fines are certain. The Central Business District is a restricted zone for private vehicles and taxis from 7:30 am. to 10:15 am. (Mondays to Saturdays except public holidays). Drivers entering the zone are required to purchase and display Area Licences. Cars and taxis with four or more persons, driver included, are exempt, A daily licence can be purchased for $4 ($2 for taxis) at booths just outside the CBD zones.

Taxis

There are more than 10,000 taxis in Singapore and they come in four colour combinations: black and yellow, light blue with a red stripe, dark blue and light blue, or white and green with yellow stripe. Taxis are cheap, available and usually reliable. Only very occasionally do you have to remind them to flag down their meters.

On busy roads like **Shenton Way** during business hours, taxis will only stop at authorised taxi stands, so you are wasting your time trying to hail them in the streets. Also around 4 pm you may see a lot of empty taxis. They are changing shifts and refuse to pick up passengers. The flag fare is $1 ($1.20 for air-conditioned taxis) for the first (1.5 km.) and 10 cents for each additional 375m., with a 20 cents surcharge for every four minutes waiting time.

Tipping is not customary for taxi drivers unless they have been especially helpful.

Buses

Don't be afraid to hop on a bus. They provide both a wonderful opportunity for mixing with the local population and an economical way of sightseeing. Buses run from 6 am. to 11:30 pm. and travel along almost the same route on the outward and return journey. Buses are regular and, although not the last word in comfort, they will get you there fairly quickly. In fact on a rainy day when every taxi disappears off the face of the earth, a bus makes a good alternative.

Fares cost 40 cents for the first four stages, 50 cents for five to seven stages, 50 cents for eight to 10 stages, 70 cents for 11 to 13 stages, and 80 cents for really long journeys of over 13 stages.

Bus guides, with complete details of all the bus routes are available at 50 cents a copy at bookshops and newsstands. Or

Right, *passengers stand on a bus during traffic rush*

Left, *Cable car from Faber Hill to Sentosa Island*

you can call the **Singapore Bus Service**. Tel: 284-8866.

Mini-Buses

This is the yellow mini-bus you see zooming around town. There are eight services and they start at 6:30 am. but finish at 7:30 pm. **Service 2**: From Orchard Road down to Collyer Quay and Shenton Way and back again. **Service 3**: From Orchard Road it will take you to Chinatown (Upper Cross Street) and People's Park (New Bridge Road) and back to Orchard Boulevard. **Service 5**: From Orchard Road down to Collyer Quay, Raffles Quay and Shenton Way. **Service 7**: From Orchard Road down to Selegie Road and the Peace Centre. **Service 8**: From Shenton Way to Chinatown (Cross Street) and out to Telok Blangah Way. **Service 9**: From Collyer Quay to National Museum (Stamford Road).

CBD

If you want to get into the Central Business District during the restricted time in the morning and can't find a taxi, you may find a new bus service known as **CBD** 1 and 2 a help.

CBD 1 runs from the Handicraft Centre Centre in Tanglin Road down to Shenton Way, taking in Orchard Road, Dhoby Ghaut, Bras Basah Road, Nicoll Highway, Connaught Drive, Fullerton Road, Collyer Quay, Raffles Quay, Shenton Way and on to Anson Road and Tanjong Pagar.

CBD 2 starts from Cluny Road by the Botanic Gardens, and goes down Napier Road, Tanglin Road, Orchard Road, Dhoby Ghaut, Bras Basah Road, North Bridge Road, South Bridge Road and New Bridge Road which makes it very convenient if you want to go to People's Park.

Both services run from 9:10 am. to 5:00 pm. on weekdays and 9:10 am. to 12:20 pm. and 3:30 pm. to 8:00 pm. on Saturdays. They will not run on Sundays or public holidays. The fare is a flat rate of 40 cents.

Trishaw

The trishaw, a bicycle with a side car,

replaced the rickshaw when the Japanese occupied most of South East Asia during World War II. It is a fast disappearing Oriental mode of transportation in most cities of Asia but has been re-established in Singapore for the tourists; however, it isn't only tourists who use them. The trishaw is a fascinating way to explore the city. There is no standard fare and it is advisable to come to an agreement with the driver about the fare before starting.

Car Hire

The ideal way to see Singapore island is by hired car. (See the section, "Exploring Singapore Island.") For those who want to travel beyond, you can hire a car in Singapore and travel to Malaysia, and leave the car in **Kuala Lumpur** or **Penang**. Self-drive cars can be hired by the days or week.

A list of car hire companies can be found under "Motorcar Renting" in the Yellow Pages of the *Singapore Phone Book*.

Sampan

Sampans and luxury motor launches are available for trips around the harbour and to nearby islands. Small sampans with outboard motors gather around **Clifford Pier** and **Jardine Steps**. For transportation to and from ships in the harbour the fee is $1 per person. For longer distance prices must be negotiated.

Airlines

Singapore is serviced by some thirty International Airlines with more than 1,200 flights a week.

Aerofloat Soviet Airlines
110-112 Shaw Centre, Scotts Road.
Tel: 737-7111

Air Lanka
SIA ticketing Office, SIA Building, 77 Robinson Road.
Tel: 223-8888 Ext. 413

Air India
16th, UIC Building, Shenton Way.
Tel: 220-5277

Air New Zealand
Ocean Building, Ground floor, Collyer Quay.
Tel: 918-266

Alitalia
10th floor, Liat Towers, Orchard Road.
Tel: 737-3166

Biman, Airlines of Bangladesh
13th floor, Straits Trading Building, Battery Road.
Tel: 915-116

Braniff Airways
101 Tanglin Shopping Centre, 19 Tanglin Road.
Tel: 734-7321

British Airways
International Building, Orchard Road.
Tel: 737-1422

Burma Airways
c/o Singapore Airlines, SIA Building, Robinson Road.
Tel: 222-1111

Cathay Pacific Airways
Ocean Building, Ground Floor, Collyer Quay.
Tel: 911-411

China Airlines
2nd floor, Lucky Plaza, Orchard Road.
Tel: 737-3208

Czechoslovak Airlines
3rd floor, Holiday Inn, Suite 5, Scotts Road.
Tel: 737-9844

Garuda Indonesian Airways
Wisma Indonesia, Orchard Road.
Tel: 737-0693

Japan Air Lines
1st floor, Hong Leong Building, Raffles Quay.
Tel: 220-2211

KLM Royal Dutch Airlines
G2, Mandarin Hotel Arcade, Orchard Road.
Tel: 737-7622

Korean Airlines
Ocean Building, Ground floor.
Tel: 917-611

Lufthansa German Airlines
Tanglin Shopping Centre, Ground floor,
Tanglin Road.
Tel: 737-9222

Malaysian Airlines System
53 Anson Center, Anson Road.
Tel: 220-2011
olympic airwaysHoliday Inn Building,
Scoots Road.
Tel:737-4088

Pakistan International Airlines
Thong Teck Building, Scotts Road.
Tel: 737-3233

Pan American World Airways (Pan Am)
Hong Leong Building, Robinson Road.
Tel: 220-0711

Philippine Air Lines
G-10, Park Lane Shopping Maul, Selegie
Road.
Tel: 320-113

Qantas Airways
Mandarin Hotel Arcade, Orchard Road.
Tel: 737-3744

Royal Brunei Airlines
10th floor, Orchard Towers, Orchard
Road.
Tel: 235-4672

Sabena Belgium World Airlines
International Plaza, Ground floor, Anson
Road.
Tel: 221-7054

Scandinavian Airlines System
Finlayson House, Raffles Quay.
Tel: 919-877

Singapore Airlines
SIA Building, Robinson Road.
Tel: 222-1111

*Old house on Beach Road stands in
contrast to the Merlin Hotel*

Swissair
1st floor, Lucky Plaza, Orchard Road.
Ṭel: 737-8133

Thai Airways International
Finlayson House, Raffles Quay.
Tel: 919-877

UTA French Airlines
Ming Court Hotel, Tanglin Road.
Tel: 737-7166

Yugoslav Airlines
6th floor, 610 Far East Shopping Centre,
Orchard Road.
Tel: 235-3017

Tourist Hotels

Ambassador Hotel. 167 rooms
42-46 Meyer Road, Singapore 1543.
Tel: 446-3311
Single $79.10; Double $90.40; Suites
$203.40
24-hour coffee shop; poolside beer
garden; cocktail lounge, Chinese
restaurant and night club; quiet district
facing the sea.

Apollo Hotel. 343 rooms
405 Havelock Road, Singapore 3016.
Tel: 432-081
Single $120; Double $140; Suites $220
Coffee shop; theatre restaurant and night
club; Japanese restaurant; Indonesian
restaurant; bar.

Asia, Hotel. 140 rooms
37 Scotts Road, Singapore 0922.
Tel: 737-8388
Single $90; Double $110; Suites $150
Coffee shop; cocktail lounge with live
entertain.

Century Park Sheraton. 464 rooms
Nassim Hill, Singapore 1025.
Tel: 737-9677
Single $180; Double $200; Suites from
$350-500
24-hour coffee shop; cocktail lounge;

*Hugo's famous Continental restaurant in
the Hyatt; centre, doormen at the Ming
Court; right, pretty waitress at the
Hilton's poolside Tradewinds Bar*

discotheque; European and Japanese restaurants; health centre; pool.

Cockpit Hotel. 220 rooms
6-7 Oxley Rise, Singapore 0923.
Tel: 737-9111
Single $105; Double $120; Suites $200
Georgian style 15-storey building. Restaurants; coffee shop, lounges; night club; shopping arcade; swimming pool.

Equatorial, Hotel. 224 rooms
429 Bukit Timah, Singapore 1025.
Tel: 256-0431
Single $110; Double $125; Suite from $130-144
Restaurants; pool; shopping arcade; few minutes to city centre

Goodwood Park Hotel. 300 rooms
22 Scotts Road, Singapore 0922.
Tel: 737-7411
Single $155; Double $175; Suites from $300
On 14-acre site, 10 minutes from downtown. Two pools; restaurants; playground for children. Golf nearby.

Grand Central, Hotel. 150 rooms
Kramat Lane, Singapore 0922.
Tel: 737-9944
Single $90; Double $105; Suite $115
Coffee shop; cocktail lounge; Omei restaurant; good location off Orchard Road.

Hilton International Singapore. 480 rooms
581 Orchard Road, Singapore 0923.
Tel: 737-2233
Single $135; Double $160; Suite from $325
Twenty-six storey high rise with rooftop pool amidst tropical surrounding, adjoining lounge and restaurant, nightly entertainment.

Holiday Inn. 600 rooms
25 Scotts Road, Singapore 0922.
Tel: 737-7966
Single $140; Double $220; Suite $170-210
In the centre of entertainment district. Pool; health club with sauna; department store next door; two bars; 24-hour Cafe

Vienna.

Hyatt Regency Hotel. 824 rooms
10 Scotts Road, Singapore 0922.
Tel: 737-5511
Single $135-185; Double $170-220; Suite from $270-1000
Another huge highrise, 10 minutes from downtown. All facilities, including shopping arcade and pool.

Mandarin Singapore. 1200 rooms
333 Orchard Road, Singapore 0923.
Tel: 737-4411
Single $155-225; Double $185-275; Suite from $300-1200
Tallest and most central, only Singapore hotel with roof-top revolving restaurant. Five cocktail lounges; eight nightclubs and restaurants; shopping acrade; television.

Marco Polo, Singapore. 603 rooms
127 Tanglin Road, Singapore 1024.
Tel: 474-7141
Single $140: Double $170; Suite from $270-350
Spacious rooms and suites with individual air conditioning control, coloured T.V.; refrigerator; open-air swimming pool; two restaurants; 24-hour coffee shop; first-class discotheque.

Merlin Hotel. 354 rooms
Beach Road, Singapore 0719.
Tel: 258-0011
Single $110, Double $125; Suite $270-350
Restaurants; bar with entertainment.

Metropole Hotel. 54 rooms
41 Seah Street, Singapore 0718.
Tel: 336-3611
Single $75; Double $90; Suite $160-195
Cocktail lounge; night club; coffee shop and Chinese restaurant.

Ming Court Hotel. 299 rooms
Tanglin Road, Singapore 1024.
Tel: 737-1133
Single $145; Double $165; Suite from $200
24-hour coffee shop; Chinese restaurant; French restaurant; cocktail lounge; swimming pool; shopping arcade;

excellent location.

Miramar, Hotel. 214 rooms
401 Havelock Road, Singapore 0316.
Tel: 910-222
Single $95; Double $110; Suite from $120
Sixteen stories in garden setting, five minutes from downtown. Clubs; pool and shopping arcade.

Oberoi, Imperial Hotel. 600 rooms
1 Jalan Rumbia, Singapore 0923.
Tel: 737-666
Single $140; Double $155; Suite from $250
Centrally located, 600 rooms scattered on 13 floors, all with 4-channel music systems, telephones and air-conditioning; 4 restaurants; 2 bars; pool with terrace;

arcade and shops

Peninsula Hotel. 315 rooms
Coleman Street, Singapore 0617.
Tel: 337-8091
Single $108; Double $124; Suite $220
Located in the heart of the city's commercial and entertainment centre; 4 restaurants.

Phoenix Hotel. 300 rooms
Somerset Road, Singapore 0923.
Tel: 737-8666
Single $88-108; Double $99-124; Suite from $145-185
4 restaurants, including an open-air roof

Chef at the Marco Polo restaurant

garden restaurant. Near the Specialists' Centre.

Raffles Hotel. 127 rooms
1-3 Beach Road, Singapore 0178.
Tel: 337-8041
Single $155; Double $175; Suite from $200
Huge rooms, mellow with age but comfortable and full of nostalgia, for Colonial period; Prestige place; Steak house.

Royal Ramada Hotel. 321 rooms
36, Newton Road, Singapore 1130.
Tel: 253-4411
Single $25-95; Double $90-110; Suite $150-600
Sixteen storey highrise near exclusive residential district; restaurants; pool; shops.

Sea View Hotel. 420 rooms
10 Amber Close, Singapore 1543.
Tel: 446-1122
Single $70-85; Double $85-100; Suites $150
Restaurants; Cocktail lounge; coffee-shop

Shangri-La Hotel. 700 rooms
22 Orange Grove, Singapore 1025.
Tel: 737-3644
Single $140-160; Double $170-190; Suite from $320-370
On 12.5 acre garden site. Tennis courts; pool; club; disco; 3-hole golf course.

Singapura Forum Hotel. 193 rooms
585 Orchard Road, Singapore 0923.
Tel: 737-1122
Single $95; Double $120; Suite $180
Coffee house; bars; pool; Szechuan restaurant and arcade.

Tai-Pan Hotel. 269 rooms
101 Victoria Street, Singapore 0718.
Tel: 366-811
Single $80-95; Double $90-105; Suite from $125-400
Tim Sum Chinese restaurant; cocktail lounge; grill room; 24-hour coffee shop. Good location with overlooking harbour.

York Hotel. 401 rooms
21 Mount Elizabeth, Singapore 0922.
Tel: 737-0511
Single $105-145; Double $125-165; Suite $170-250
Cocktail lounge; coffee house; rooftop grill; bar; pool; sauna; beauty and barber shops.

"Backpackers" Hotels
Small, inexpensive Chinese hotels in Singapore are plentiful but are scattered from Chinatown to the outlying districts. Not all of them are listed in the phone books. Generally they are noisy with paper-thin walls and the electric light may be a naked bulb in a socket hanging from the centre of the ceiling. But if you are looking for atmosphere, and travelling on a tight budget, the Chinese hotels may be the way to go. Some Chinese hotels cater only to Chinese so don't be surprised if you are turned away. However, around **Beach Road** and **Bencoolen Street** there are several hotels favoured by backpackers. Government taxes are usually included and there are no 10 per cent service charges. The difference between economy and first class is an air-conditioning unit stuck in the window. Don't expect sheets and towels to be changed daily. Not all hotels listed here are Chinese.

Bencoolen Hotel. 69 rooms
47 Bencoolen Street, Singapore 0718.
Tel: 337-5282
Rooms air-conditioned; Single $47.50; Double $53.80 This is one of the bigger Chinese hotels.

Hai Chew Lodging House. 12 rooms
35 Beach Road, Singapore 0718.
Tel: 388-0578
Rooms air-conditioned; Single $14; Double $18

Hai Hin Hotel. 20 rooms
97-A Beach Road, Singapore 0718.
Tel: 338-0578
Rooms air-conditioned; Single $16; Double $20

Kian Hua Hotel. 20 rooms
81 Bencoolen Street, Singapore 0718.
Tel: 338-3492
Rooms airconditioned; Single $15;

Double $18, $20, $22

San Wah Hotel. 11 rooms
36 Bencoolen Street, Singapore 0718.
Tel: 362-428
Rooms without air-conditioning; Single $26; Double $28
Rooms air-conditioned; Single $24; Double $26

Shang Onn Hotel. 10 rooms
37 Beach Road, Singapore 0718.
Tel: 338-4153
Rooms without air-conditioning; Single $18; Double $20

Station Hotel. 34 rooms
Keppel Road, Singapore 0208.
Tel: 222-1551
Rooms with air-conditioning; Single $34; Double $43

Tiong Hoa Hotel. 14 rooms
4 Prinsep Street, Singapore 0718.
Tel: 338-4522
Rooms without air-conditioning; Single $31; Double $35

Metropolitan YMCA. 50 rooms
70 Palmer Road, Singapore 0207.
Tel: 222-4666
Rooms with air-conditioning; Single $19, With bath attached, without air-conditioning; Double $36

YMCA. 6 rooms
Orchard Road, Singapore 0923.
Tel: 337-7638
Rooms with air-conditioning; Single $24; Double $28

YWCA. 27 rooms
6, Fort Canning Road, Singapore 0617.
Tel: 361-212
Rooms air-conditioned with bath attached; Single $31; Double $39

Cinemas

In this small republic where strip shows and juke boxes are illegal and *Playboy* magazine is banned from the streets, the censors make havoc of imported films dealing with sex and violence. But nevertheless, the average Singaporean is

Chinese opera above *appeals more to older Chinese while the majority of Singaporeans relish a good romantic movie,* left

an avid moviegoer. The island boasts 67 cinemas. Admission prices are inexpensive: $1.50, $2.50 and $3.50. Listed below are a few of the first-class cinemas that show Western movies.

Capital Theatre
Box Office, North Bridge Road.
Tel: 329-795

Cathay Organisation Pte. Ltd
Dhoby Ghaut, Cathay Building.
Tel: 330-400

Lido Theatre
Box Office, Orchard Road.
Tel: 737-3414

Odeon Theatre
Box Office, 331 North Bridge Road.
Tel: 321-116

Orchard Theatre
Box Office, Grange Road.
Tel: 737-6588

Rex Theatre
Box Office, 2 MacKenzie Road.
Tel: 34-042

Banks and Business Contacts

Singapore is rapidly becoming the banking capital of Southeast Asia. The republic has 81 banks with 271 offices, 77 merchant banks and three discount houses. Banks in Singapore operate under the supervision and control of the Monetary Authority of Singapore. Visitors are advised to be careful when changing their money in shops, and when using street money-changers not to accept any currency but Singapore dollars for local use.

Local currency in circulation is denominated in Singapore dollars and cents. Paper currency is available in

Left, dancer at the Neptune Theatre and right, night traffic in front of the Capitol Theatre on Stamford Road

denomination of $1, $5, $10, $25, $50, $100, $500, $1,000 and $10,000. Coins are 1 cents, 10 cents, 20 cents, 50 cents and $1.

Normal banking hours are from 10 am. to 3 pm. on weekdays and from 9:30 am. to 11.30 am. on Saturdays. Banks do not have foreign exchange dealings on Saturdays.

Money Changers

Besides banks, there are many money changers operating in town from whom you can buy or sell currency. For your own protection, deal only with licenced money changers. The rates offered by them are slightly better than those obtainable at banks. You can find them at **Change Alley, Raffles Place** and some of the major shopping centres.

Business Contact

Visitors in need of legal advice or assistance should contact their own embassies or consulates. Businessmen seeking secretarial and telephone answering services may contact **Communicate Private Limited**, Suite 1404, Shaw Towers, Beach Road, Telephone: 2931-577. Office-on-the-wire provides 24 hour private and confidential secretarial service, telex exchange and mail collecting and forwarding and courier services. Temporary office space and business consultancy are also available.

Languages, Newspapers, Radio and TV

Malay is Singapore's national language, but less than half the population speak it; English is the language of the courts and administration, but not everyone knows it; Mandarin is spoken on TV and over radio news broadcasts yet the main Chinese dialects are Hokkien, Teochew, Cantonese, Hainanese, Hakka and Foochow. But the dialects are not only Chinese. There are Telegu, Malayalam, Punjabi, Hindu and Bengali. Emphasis now in Singapore is to do away with Chinese dialects and speak Mandarin.

But English is still the major language and everyone but sampan boys and island fisherfolk will speak it, although it has taken on its own form of Singapore dialect — *lah*!

Communication in such a diverse language media presents many problems. Aside from the radio broadcasting in six different languages, there are 10 daily newspapers: Four Chinese, three English, two Tamil, one Malay and one Malayalam.

Embassies and Consulates

Most foreign missions in Singapore are closed on Saturdays, many open only in the mornings even on weekdays, so it's advisable to check office hours before you make a visit.

Arab Republic of Egypt
20-C/22-C, Patterson Road.
Tel: 737-1811

Argentina
L-1, 11th floor, International Building, Orchard Road.
Tel: 235-4231.

Australia
25, Napier Road.
Tel: 737-9311

Austria
2004/5, 20th floor, Shaw Centre, Scotts Road.
Tel: 235-4088

Bangladesh
Unit 206, 2nd floor, Dunn House, 90 Cecil Street.
Tel: 220-9015

Britain
Tanglin Road.
Tel: 639-333

Burma
15 St. Martin's Drive.
Tel: 235-8763

Canada
8th floor, Faber House, Orchard Road.
Tel: 737-1322

China (Republic of)
Trade Mission, 13th floor, UIC Building,

Shenton Way.
Tel: 222-4951

Denmark
815 Supreme House, Penang Road.
Tel: 336-2488

France
5 Gallop Road.
Tel: 664-866

Germany (Federal Republic of)
12th floor, Far East Shopping Centre.
Tel: 737-6809

Greece
Room 707, 7th floor, Robina House,
Shenton Way.
Tel: 220-8622

India
31 Grange Road.
Tel: 737-1355

Indonesia
435 Orchard Road.
Tel: 737-7422

Ireland
c/o Godwin & Company, 19th floor,
Straits Trading Bldg, Battery Road.
Tel: 916-377

Israel
230-K, 10th floor, Faber House, Orchard
Road.
Tel: 235-0966

Italy
Room 811, 8th floor, Supreme House,
Penang Road.
Tel: 337-1178

Japan
16 Nassim Road.
Tel: 235-8855

Korea (Republic of)
2408-14 24th floor, Shaw Centre, Scotts
Road.
Tel: 737-6411

Malaysia
301 Jervois Road.
Tel: 235-0111

Netherlands
12th floor, Liat Towers, Orchard Road.
Tel: 737-1155

New Zealand
13 Nassim Road.
Tel: 235-9966

Norway
16th floor, Hong Leong Building, Raffles
Quay.
Tel: 220-7122

Pakistan
Room 510, 5th floor, Shaw House,
Orchard Road.
Tel: 737-6988

Panama
Room 3906, 39th floor, Hong Leong
Building, Raffles Quay.
Tel: 221-8677

Philippines
Room 505-506, 5th floor, Thong Teck
Building, Scotts Road.
Tel: 737-3977

Poland
Suite 2308/2312, 23rd floor, Shaw
Towers, Beach Road.
Tel: 294-2513/4

Romania
64 Sime Road.
Tel: 468-3424

Saudi Arabia
10 Nassim Road.
Tel: 734-5878

Spain
26th floor, CPF Building, 79 Robinson
Road.
Tel: 220-4222

Sri Lanka
Room 1207-1212, Goldhill Plaza,
Newton Road.
Tel: 254-4595

Sweden
4th floor, PUB Building, Devonshire
Wing, Somerset Road.
Tel: 734-2771

Switzerland
Room 1703/04 Liat Towers, Orchard
Road.
Tel: 737-4666

Thailand
370 Orchard Road.
Tel: 737-2644

U.S.A.
30 Hill Street.
Tel: 338-0251

U.S.S.R.
51 Nassim Road.Tel: 235-1834

Yogoslavia
52 Stevens Road.
Tel: 252-5755

Clubs and Associations

Want to know where the best areas are around Singapore to go scuba diving, when the next cricket match is scheduled or where you can see a polo game? Or maybe you have a yearning to go sky diving over Singapore. A local club may be your answer. Listed here are a few of Singapore's popular private clubs:

Alliance Francaise
4 Draycott Park
Tel: 737-8422

American Club
21 Scotts Road.
Tel: 373-3411

Aquanaut Club, Singapore
Suite 1414, Shaw Towers.
Tel: 2934-211

Automobile Association of Singapore
A.A. House, 450 River Valley Road.
Tel: 737-0633

Cricket Club, Singapore
Esplanade.
Tel: 338-9271

Deutsches Haus
21 First Avenue.
Tel: 669-548

Japanese Association
34 Scotts Road.
Tel: 737-3611

Top, *night crowd at Temple Street;*
centre, *raw fish delicacies; curb-side stall*

Lions Club
Room 26, 3rd floor, Meyer Chambers,
Raffles Place.
Tel: 430-207

Masonic Club
26 A, Coleman Street.
Tel: 336-0052

Parachute Association of Singapore
School of Commando Training, Changi.
Tel: 545-1551 Ext. 620/8

Polo Club, Singapore
Thompson Road.
Tel: 256-4530

Red Cross House
15 Penang Lane.
Tel: 323-587

Rotary Club
F-15, 3rd floor, Mandarin Hotel,
Orchard Road.
Tel: 737-2504

Skal Club
122 Serangoon Road.
Tel: 880-376

Swimming Club, Singapore
Tanjong Rhu.
Tel: 446-2122

Swiss Club
192 Swiss Club Road.
Tel: 663-270

Tanglin Club
5 Stevens Road.
Tel: 737-6011

Young Mens Christian Association
"A" Orchard Road.
Tel: 337-7638

Young Womens' Christian Association
211 Colombo Court.
Tel: 336-3929

National Museum and Art Gallery

Originally established at its present site in
Stamford Road in 1887 as a museum of
natural history and anthropology, the
National Museum was known as the
Raffles Museum until 1960. Two hours in
the museum and a visitor will have a
better understanding of Southeast Asian
history. The earliest known Chinese trade
routes are shown on wall maps and
charts, and pieces of pottery depicting
these early trade routes are also on
display. The museum is devoted to the
art, history, and ethnology of Singapore
and Southeast Asia. Displays include
items of prehistoric archaeology, Malay
weapons, silverware and fabrics, Chinese
porcelain, coins and currency of the
region from the earliest times, cultural
materials of West Malaysian aborigines,
Chinese furniture and costumes.

Housed in the same building is the
museum's art gallery. On display are
contemporary paintings and sculptures.
Also on display is the collection of art of
the University of Singapore. Students' art
and crafts are in the Young People's
Gallery. Open daily, including Sundays
and public holidays from 10:30 am. to 7
pm. Admission is free.

National Library

For the researcher and serious student of
Southeast Asian studies, the National
Library offers some of the best facilities
in Southeast Asia. Aside from one and
half million books listed, there are also
books in braille, large print books, music
scores, microfilms and microfiches, as
well as a collection of maps and
photographs. It also provides photo-
copying services and a variety of cultural,
recreational and educational programmes
for children, young people and adults.

Tour Agent

The Singapore Tourist Promotion
Board has licensed 371 tourist agencies in
Singapore. Before dealing with any
agencies make sure they are associate
members of STPB. The list here does not
necessarily include the biggest tourist
agencies in Singapore, but they do handle
the largest volume of local tours.

American Express
Travel Division, Holiday Inn Building.
Tel: 737-5988

Anglo-French Travel
9th floor, Asia Chambers, 29 McCallum
Street.
Tel: 222-8111

Associated Tours
904 Wellington Building.
Tel: 235-7222

Garden City Associates
315 & 317 Blk A, Merlin Plaza.
Tel: 258-0305

Harpers Travel (Tour East)
5 Shenton Way, 17th floor, UIC
Building.
Tel: 220-2200

Holiday Tours and Travel
Mezzine floor, 10-14 Ming Court Hotel,
Shopping Arcade.
Tel: 737-0533

Nandas Travel
39 Stamford Road, Room 121 & 122, 1st
floor.
Tel: 320-343

Orient Explorer
Stamford House, Room 225.
Tel: 337-6136

Prime Tours
2002 Shaw Centre, 20th FLoor.
Tel: 235-3222

Siakson Coach Tours
24/32 Prinsep Street.Tel: 30-276
Tel: 336-0288

Sita World Travel
69 Raffles Hotel, Beach Road.
Tel: 338-3812

Sito Tours
4th floor, 322 Merlin Plaza, Beach Road.
Tel: 292-5068

Thomas Cook
903-904 Orchard Towers.
Tel: 737-0366

Travel Centre of Singapore
Lobby, Ming Court Hotel, Tanglin Road.
Tel: 737-3440

Universal Travel Corporation
B66, People's Park Centre.
Tel: 915-577

World Express
Suite 69, Raffles Hotel, Beach Road.
Tel: 336-3877

What to Wear

Dress is normally very casual so pack
light summer clothing (preferably of
natural fabrics) and comfortable shoes or
sandals. Only a few places require formal
wear for the evening. Visitors should
phone beforehand to check. However,
suits and evening dresses are never out of
place in first-class hotels and nightspots.

Tipping

Most hotels and restaurants add a 10 per
cent service charge to the bill. Tipping
then is not necessary. In other places, a
tip of 10 per cent of the bill is normal. For
bellboy and messenger services, the tip
could range from 50 cents to $1. It's not
necessary to tip taxi drivers. The STPB is
trying to create a "Tipping Free" society.
Some hotels and restaurants discourage
tipping.

Electricity

The common voltage is 220-240 volts 50
cycles. Most hotels have a transformer to
reduce the voltage to 110-120 volts, 60
cycles, when necessary.

Drinking Water

In Singapore, the water is clean and safe
to drink from the tap. Nor do you have to
worry about iced drinks at any of the
food stalls.

Telephone Calls

Visitors can speak direct from their hotel
rooms to most principal cities in the
world. Local calls made from private
phones are free of charge. Calls made
from pay phones cost 10 cents per call
for three minutes.

Photographic Film

Black and white film can be developed
and processed in eight hours and colour
in 24 hours. Do not send undeveloped

film in parcels through the post for it may be X-rayed.

Complaints

The Singapore Tourist Promotion Board takes prompt action when a tourist complains. If you have a complaint, against a shopkeeper for example, do not hesitate to write to the STPB, **131 Tudor Court, Tanglin Road,** or call them. Appropriate action will then be taken. If a taxi driver gives you a problem, report him to the **Registrar of Vehicles (ROV)** or call the STPB.

Jaywalking

Jaywalking is an offence in Singapore. Violation of the law is a $50 fine. Use designated crossings at cross roads, also overhead bridges, underpasses and zebra crossings. Don't think that if you are a tourist you are exempt.

Littering

A cigarette butt tossed on a street can mean a $500 fine. Singapore is undoubtedly the cleanest city in Asia, and to maintain its record the laws are stringent. Litter bins are provided everywhere. Follow the Singapore rule and use them rather than being fined.

Long Hair

At all government offices there are posters showing that long hair is out. Males with long hair are served last. The Singapore Government does not approve of identification with life styles which are not in consonance with its national values.

Drugs

Singapore is hard on drug users of any sort. Possession as well as trafficking is a serious offence. Ignorance of the law is no excuse.

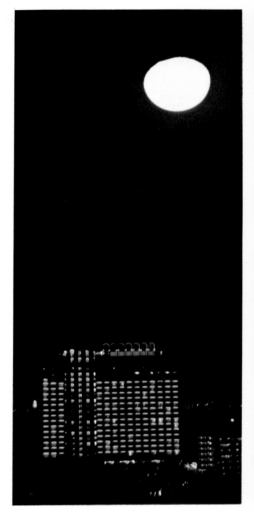

And if You Get Lost

Where else can you have it so nice! If you get lost in Singapore and can't find your way, call the **General Post Office,** Tel: 275-1911, or **The Singapore Bus Company,** Tel: 284-8866

Shangri-la Hotel